4/18

Simple
PATCHWORK
Projects

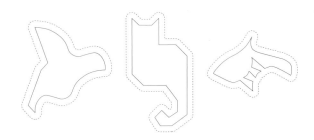

Simple
PATCHWORK
Projects

20 ANIMAL-THEMED PROJECTS TO SEW & QUILT

HAYLEY SMITH

The Taunton Press
Inspiration for hands-on living®

The Taunton Press, Inc., 63 South Main Street, PO Box 5506, Newtown, CT 06470-5506
e-mail: tp@taunton.com

Text and Illustrations: Hayley Smith
Editor: Julie Brooke
Jacket Design: Rosalind Loeb
Design and Layout: Leah Germann
Step Photography: Neil Reid
Location Photography: Mark Winwood
Location Art Direction: Simon Webb
Location courtesy of Fabulous Vintage Finds

Library of Congress Cataloging-in-Publication Data in progress
ISBN 978-1-63186-917-4

Printed in China
10 9 8 7 6 5 4 3 2 1

Contents

Introduction	**6**
Before You Begin	**8**

Cats & Dogs   10

Labrador Tote Bag	12
Cat Pillow Cover	16
Scottie Dog Bolster Pillow	20
Cat and Mouse Clock	24

Farm Animals   28

Chicken Apron	30
Sheep Play Mat	34
Cow Tea Cozy	38
Horse Wall Hanging	42

Water Creatures   46

Angelfish Brush Roll	48
Turtle Stool Cover	52
Goldfish Journal Cover	56
Penguin Hot Pad	60

Forest Animals   64

Owl Portfolio	66
Hedgehog Project Bag	70
Fox Seat Pad	74
Teddy Bear Blanket	78

Wild Animals   82

Elephant Bulletin Board	84
Monkey Tablet Sleeve	88
Lizard Seat Cushion	92
Bird Place Mat	96

Techniques   100

Index	**125**
Resources	**128**
Acknowledgments	**128**

Introduction

I have enjoyed sewing English paper-pieced patchwork since my auntie Kathy introduced me to it as a child. Three years ago, I had a eureka moment. I suddenly thought, "Why does patchwork have to be plain old hexagons? If a paper shape will tessellate, why can't I use it as a template for patchwork?" So I decided to create my own shapes.

Tessellating shapes are ones that fit together without leaving any gaps. Creating the templates for them is a careful balance of math, aesthetics and sew-ability. A lot of geometry goes into the designs, but in this book I've done all of the math for you! I have found that developing tessellated shapes that look like animals can be challenging, as the limits of what will create a repeating pattern often prevents me from creating a recognizable shape. Then, if the tessellation goes to plan and the shape looks good, I have to make sure that the shape is sew-able—there's no point creating a design that is impossible to stitch! Hopefully within this book I have struck a happy medium.

The technique of working with shaped patchwork pieces allows you to take your patchwork skills to the next level. I hope that this book will provide you with a renewed love for English paper-pieced patchwork. Plus the new shapes and different techniques will allow you to create some stunning animal-themed projects.

My first templates—the Scottie Dog (see page 20) and a jigsaw piece—were launched in November 2015 on Hochanda TV, a television shopping channel in the UK. Although Hochanda was just three months old, we sold a whole days' worth of stock in one hour! It was at that point that I knew that sewists were ready for something different, and I created more shapes to expand the range, which I named Tessepatch®. This book covers some of the animal shapes I have developed for the range.

I hope you enjoy making the projects in this book as much as I have.

Hayley Smith

Before You Begin

The patchwork projects in this book are handpieced—stitched together by hand—and a little preparation goes a long way. So, before you start your first patchwork project, here are a few things to bear in mind.

Once you have chosen the design you want to make, your thoughts will turn to the fabrics you want to use. You may have a stash of fabrics you want to dip in to, or you may plan to buy the materials you need. Patchwork purists will say that only 100 percent quilting cotton fabrics of the same weight should be used. Obviously this will give you a beautiful result. But it's also important to choose fabrics that have colors or designs that will work with the shapes of the animals. For more information on choosing fabrics, see page 106.

You can use the templates to create your own designs. All you need to do is work out how many shapes you need (see pages 16 and 108).

For the projects in this book, each patchwork piece is created using two cardboard templates—a larger cutting template, which is used to cut out the fabric pieces (see page 108), and a smaller sewing template onto which the fabric is stitched. All the cutting templates allow for a ½ in. (1.25cm) seam allowance around each shape (see page 108). I recommend using cardboard with a weight of 160gsm for templates as it is thick enough to hold its shape but not so tough that you can't get a needle through it when used for sewing templates.

The You Will Need section of each project will tell you how many of the sewing templates are required. The list of materials includes the amount of fabric required to create the projects shown. To get the most from patchwork fabric, position cutting templates on the fabric before you start to cut to make sure you have the best fit with minimum waste. Some, like the teddy bear shape (see page 78) will fit and leave no gaps, but others will have a little fabric waste, which is unavoidable due to the unusual shapes. There are a couple of tricks that you can try to make the most of your fabric: Stagger the shapes instead of placing them in rows and rotate the shapes so some of them are upside down —just be careful you don't flip the shapes over to make mirror images of the original template. Make sure the templates are always on the grain of the fabric (see page 109).

For further information about the tools, materials and techniques used in this book see Techniques (page 100).

Arrange the cutting templates on the wrong side of the fabric before you start to cut out the shapes.

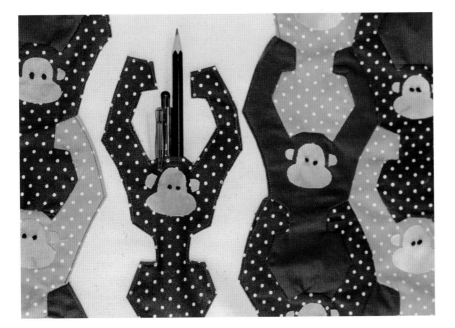

Use the patchwork shapes to create unusual features, such as the pocket on the Monkey Tablet Sleeve (see page 88).

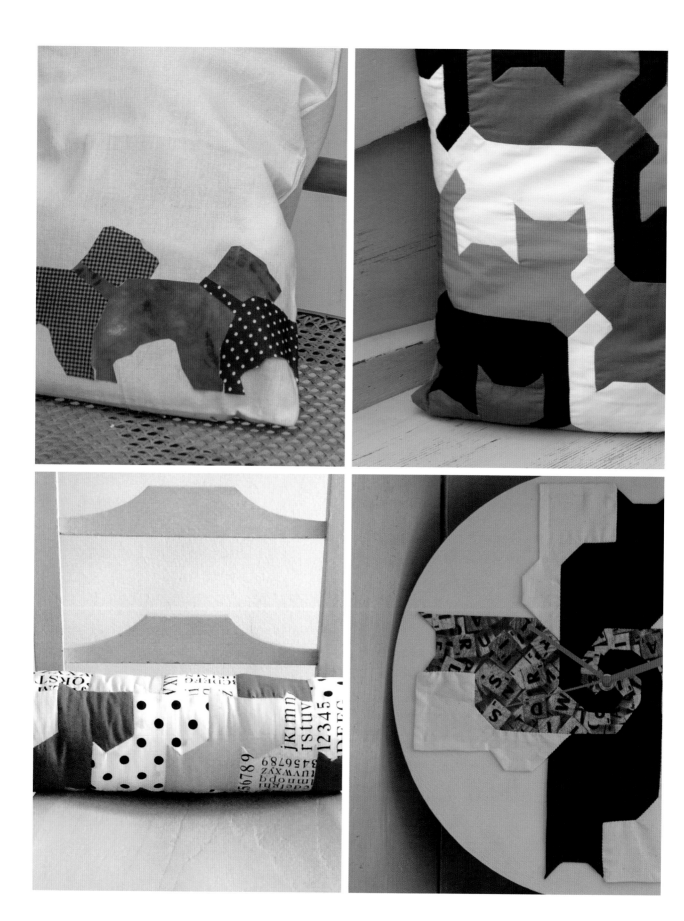

Cats & Dogs

Whether you believe that a dog will always be your best friend or that the warmest welcome home is from your pet cat, the pillows, tote bag and clock featured here will become favorite objects in your home.

Labrador Tote Bag

These delightful dogs will make your bag the talk of the town. They are a great way to use pieces from your stash. You can create a strip of patchwork to sew onto your bag, or attach the Labradors using fusible web.

You will need

8 Labrador Templates (see page 15) cut from thin cardboard or heavy paper stock (if you are using fusible web you only need 1 sewing template)

8 pieces of fabric measuring 6 x 8 in. (15 x 20cm) for the patchwork

ready-made cotton bag measuring 14 in. (35.5cm) wide

4 sheets of fusible web measuring 9 x 12 in. (23 x 30cm), if required

ruler

contrasting colored thread for basting

coordinating colored thread for sewing

coordinating embroidery floss if desired

ball-headed pins

hand-sewing needle

sewing machine, if required

Cutting out

8 Labrador shapes, 1 from each piece of fabric. If you are going to attach the dogs using fusible web, do not include a seam allowance. If you are going to sew them together, include a seam allowance and baste them to the cardboard shapes (see page 113).

Difficulty rating

Easy

Finished size

17 x 14 in. (43 x 35.5cm)

Sewing the Labrador shapes

1 Decide on the arrangement of the Labrador shapes (see page 114). With right sides facing, hand-sew 2 Labradors together. Start by joining the back of one to the front feet of another, whipstitching (see page 114) along the legs and then the tail and neck to make the collar and following the arrows on the illustration. Sew one straight seam at a time, making sure the corners are aligned. Use a coordinating colored thread and a whipstitch, and finish with a double stitch before you stitch the next section (see page 114). Then add the head to the first dog, sewing from the back of the head to the chin.

2 Continue joining Labradors to create a row of 8 dogs, adding the heads as you work. Refer to your design arrangement for color placement. Use a whipstitch and place the pieces right sides together when sewing them. Remove the basting stitches and pieces of cardboard and press the dogs on the wrong side, folding the seam allowances to the back.

Tip

If your bag is more than 14 in. (35.5cm) wide, work out how many dogs fit around the bottom edge. Measure the width of the bag. Each dog is 3½ in. (9cm) wide and so the circumference of the bag must be divisible by this (e.g. a 21-in. [53.5cm] circumference bag will require 6 dogs). Alternatively, adjust the circumference of the bag by taking in the side seams.

continued on page 14

Sewing the Labrador shapes

3 Position the row of Labradors along the bottom of one side of the bag 2–3 in. (5–7cm) from the bottom. Pin then baste in place on one side of the bag. Whipstitch the Labradors to the bag. Remove the basting stitches. Attach the row of Labradors to the other side of the bag in the same way.

Fusing the Labrador shapes

4 Arrange 4 dogs along the bottom edge of one side of the bag 2–3 in. (5–7cm) from the bottom to check that they fit around the width and align correctly with each other.

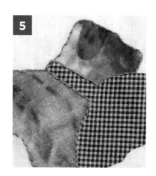

5 For a simple hand-finished effect, decorate the Labradors by embroidering the outlines with backstitch using a coordinating embroidery floss (see page 123). Alternatively, use contrasting colors and running stitch (see page 123).

6 Following the package instructions, use fusible web to attach the dogs to the bottom edge of the bag on both sides.

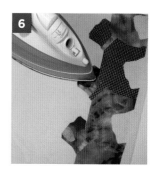

Finishing off

7 Once all the dogs are attached to the bag, embroider the edges to decorate them, if desired.

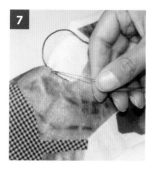

Tip

Before you sew the dogs to the bag, you may find it helpful to insert a piece of cardboard into the bag to prevent you from accidentally stitching through both layers of fabric.

Labrador Templates

Template shown at 100%

For information about cutting
out the template and fabric
shapes, see pages 109–111.

Fabric cutting line
- - - - - - -

Template cutting line
_____

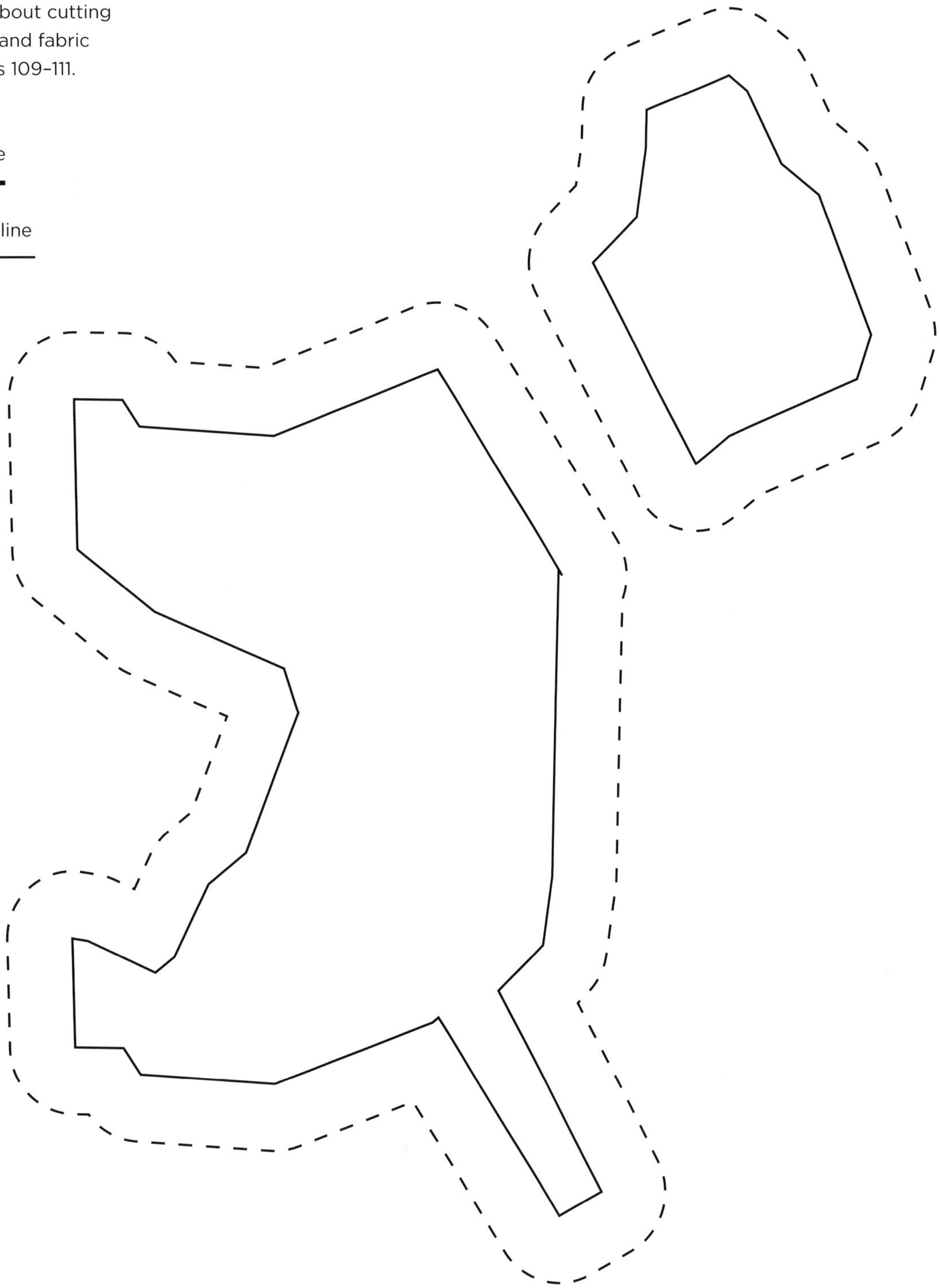

Cat Pillow Cover

A welcoming pillow decorated with a cluster of cats brings a feline theme to a favorite chair. The bright orange fabric contrasts with the black, white and gray to create this eye-catching design.

You will need

20 Cat Templates (see page 19) cut from thin cardboard or heavy paper stock

4 pieces of fabric measuring 14 x 18 in. (35.5 x 45cm) for the patchwork

1 piece of fabric measuring 20 x 30 in. (50 x76cm) for the pillow back

18-in. (45cm) square pillow form insert

tailor's chalk or erasable fabric pen

ruler

contrasting colored thread for basting

coordinating colored thread for sewing

ruler

ball-headed pins

hand-sewing needle

sewing machine

Cutting out

20 cat shapes, 5 from each fabric. Baste these to the cardboard shapes (see page 113).

One 20-in. (50cm) square and one 12 x 20-in. (30 x 50cm) rectangle from the backing fabric.

Difficulty rating

Intermediate

Finished size

18 in. (45cm) square

Sewing the cat shapes

1 Decide on the arrangement of the cat shapes (see page 114). Hand-sew the cats together in pairs, right sides together, starting with the heads. Sew the tip of one cat's tail to the neck of the other cat, following the direction of the arrow on the illustration. Use a coordinating colored thread and a whipstitch, and finish with a double stitch (see page 114).

2 Next align the bottom corner of one cat's tail with the leg of another cat, right sides together, and hand-sew this seam as before. Continue to hand-sew pairs together, following the direction of the arrow on the illustration and making sure the corners of each piece are aligned. Work a double stitch before you stitch the next section.

3 When you have sewn 18 cats together in pairs, hand-sew the pairs together to create 3 columns of 6 cats. Refer to your design arrangement for color placement. Whipstitch along the bottom of each pair with right sides together. Then use the same technique to join the columns along the long edges to make a square that is 3 cats wide by 6 cats long. The patchwork panel should measure approximately 20 in. (50cm) square. Iron the back so that the panel lies flat.

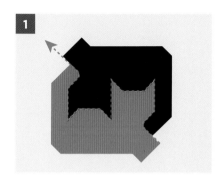

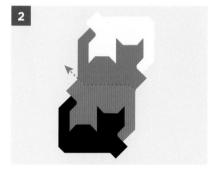

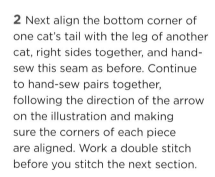

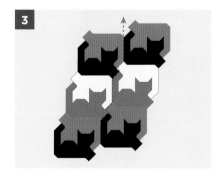

continued on page 18

Making the cover

4 Place the patchwork panel right side up on a work surface and use a ruler and tailor's chalk or an erasable fabric pen to mark a 20-in. (50cm) square in the center of the panel. If there are any gaps, cut out sections from the 2 remaining cats and use them to fill the spaces. Trim the panel along the marked lines. Remove the basting stitches and pieces of cardboard. Press the seams open on the wrong side.

5 Use a sewing machine to stitch a double-turned hem (see page 120) along one 20-in. (50cm) edge of both pieces of fabric for the pillow backing, using a 1¼-in. (3cm) seam allowance.

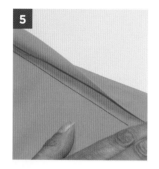

6 Place the cat panel on a work surface, right side up. Arrange the smaller backing piece on top, with the right side facing down and the unhemmed long edge aligned with the top edge of the cat panel. Then place the larger backing piece on top of the others, with the right side facing down and the unhemmed long edge aligned with the bottom edge of the cat panel. Pin the layers together.

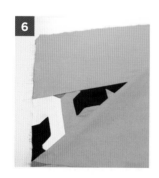

7 Use a sewing machine to stitch around all four sides of the pillow cover, leaving a 1-in. (2.5cm) seam allowance (see Assembling the Pillow Cover on the facing page). Sew the seam with the cat panel facing up to allow you to keep the patchwork seams open.

8 Trim the seam allowance to ⅜ in. (1cm), and trim the corners so that they will create sharp points when the cover is turned right side out. Iron the seams flat.

Finishing off

9 Turn the pillow cover right side out and insert the pillow form.

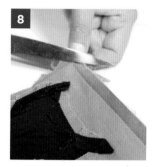

Tip

Try using the point of a bamboo skewer or knitting needle to push out the corners of the pillow cover to make them really crisp.

Cat Template

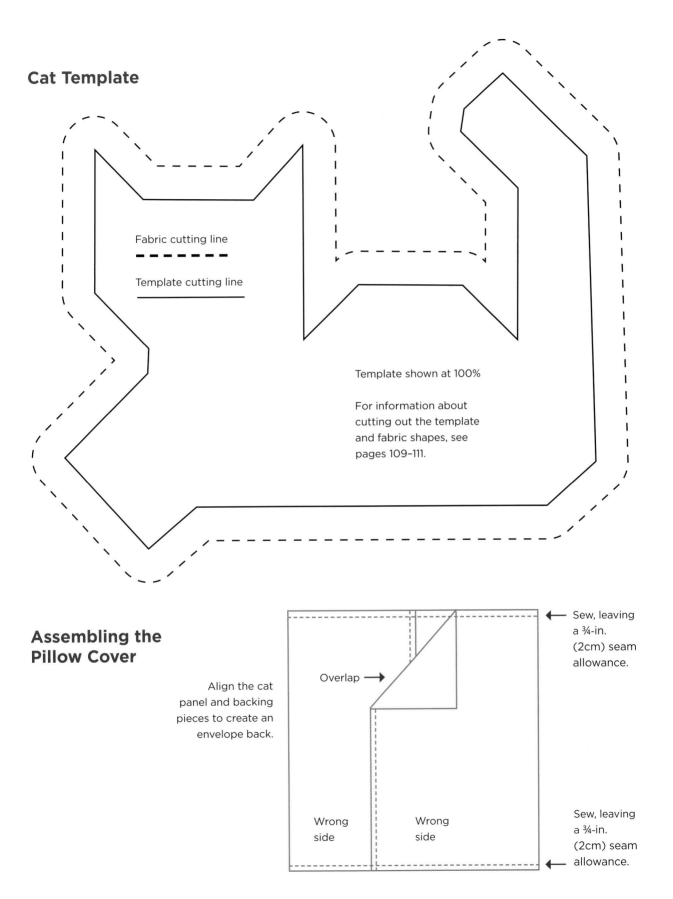

Fabric cutting line

– – – – – –

Template cutting line

————————

Template shown at 100%

For information about cutting out the template and fabric shapes, see pages 109–111.

Assembling the Pillow Cover

Align the cat panel and backing pieces to create an envelope back.

Overlap →

Sew, leaving a ¾-in. (2cm) seam allowance.

Wrong side

Wrong side

Sew, leaving a ¾-in. (2cm) seam allowance.

Scottie Dog Bolster Pillow

A favorite armchair needs a soft pillow, and this one provides the perfect back support. Plus the Scottie dog motif will bring a smile to your face whenever you see it.

You will need

18 Scottie Dog Templates (see page 23) cut from thin cardboard or heavy paper stock

4 pieces of fabric measuring 12 x 12 in. (30 x 30cm) for the patchwork

2 pieces of fabric measuring 7 x 7 in. (25 x 17.75cm) for the ends of the pillow

1 lb. 2 oz. (500g) fiberfill

2 buttons measuring 1 in. (2.5cm) in diameter

tailor's chalk or erasable fabric pen

ruler

contrasting colored thread for basting

coordinating colored thread for sewing

ball-headed pins

hand-sewing needle

sewing machine

Cutting out

18 dog shapes, 4 from 2 of the fabrics and 5 from the remaining 2 fabrics. Baste them to the cardboard shapes (see page 113).

Two 6-in. (15cm) diameter circles for the ends of the pillow.

Difficulty rating

Intermediate

Finished size

16½ x 4½ in. (41.5 x 11cm)

Sewing the dog shapes

1 Decide on the arrangement of the dog shapes (see page 114). Hand-sew the dogs together in pairs, right sides together, starting at the toes and stitching toward the ears. Sew the tip of one dog's front leg to the heel of the second dog's back leg following the direction of the arrow on the illustration. Use a coordinating colored thread and a whipstitch, and finish with a double stitch (see page 114).

2 When you have sewn the 18 dogs together in pairs, hand-sew the pairs together to create 3 rows of 6 dogs. Refer to your design arrangement for color placement. Whipstitch along the sides of each shape with right sides together.

3 Then use the same technique to join the rows along the top and bottom edges to make a patchwork panel that is 6 dogs wide by 3 dogs tall. The patchwork panel should measure approximately 16 x 31 in. (40 x 78cm). Iron the back so that the panel lies flat.

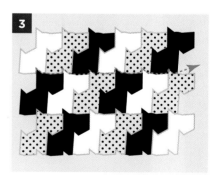

continued on page 22

Making the cover

4 Place the patchwork panel wrong side up on a work surface and use a ruler and tailor's chalk or an erasable fabric pen to mark a straight line along the long edges of the patchwork panel so that you have a rectangle measuring 17¼ x 9½ in. (44 x 24cm). Trim the panel along the marked lines.

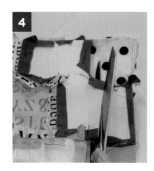

5 Fold the patchwork panel in half lengthwise with right sides facing and hand-sew the long edges together to make a cylinder, joining the ears of the dogs on the top row to the toes of the dogs on the bottom row. Use a whipstitch as before and a ¼-in. (0.5cm) seam allowance. Remove the basting stitches and pieces of cardboard. Press on the wrong side with the seams open.

6 Position one of the fabric circles against one end of the cylinder with right sides facing. Pin in position. Use a sewing machine to stitch the seam (see page 120) using a ¾-in. (2cm) seam allowance.

7 Repeat step 6 at the other end of the cylinder, leaving a 3-in. (7.5cm) gap in the seam. Press the seams open.

8 Turn the pillow cover right side out. Insert the fiberfill until the pillow is the required density. Tuck in the raw edges of the fabric and hand-sew the gap closed using a ladder stitch and a coordinating colored thread (for clarity, a contrasting colored thread has been used for the photograph).

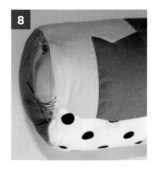

Finishing off

9 Hand-sew a button to each end of the bolster pillow using a coordinating colored thread (for clarity, a contrasting colored thread has been used for the photograph).

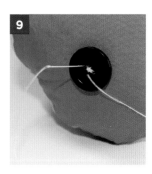

Tip

To create a template for the circles at the end of the pillow, use a plate or other object that is 6 in. (15cm) in diameter or use a pair of compasses.

Scottie Dog Template

Template shown at 100%

For information about cutting out the template and fabric shapes, see pages 109–111.

Fabric cutting line

Template cutting line

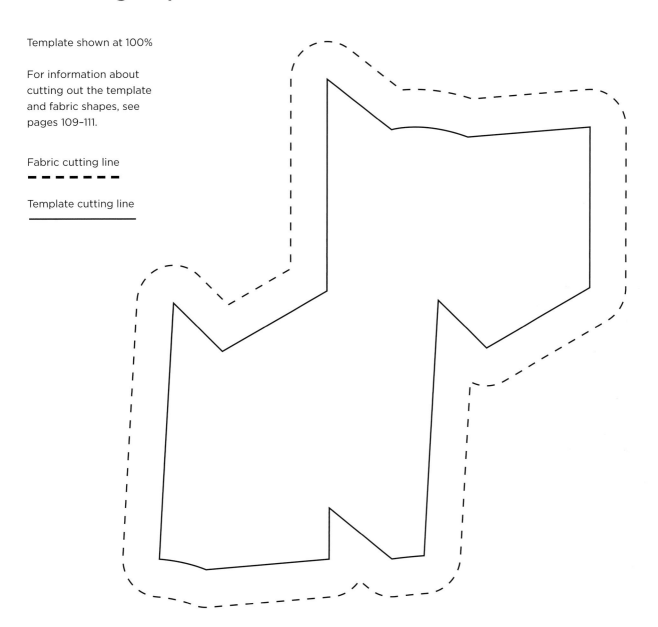

Cat and Mouse Clock

The quartet of cats on this clock face are joined by a tiny mouse that is scurrying toward the hole in the wall that leads to its home. You can leave the clock face undecorated or add numerals.

You will need

4 Cat, 4 Spacer, 1 Mouse, 1 Mouse Ear, and 1 Mouse Hole Templates (see page 27) cut from thin cardboard or heavy paper stock

3 pieces of fabric measuring 12 in. (30cm) square for the cats and spacers

Scrap of gray fabric for the mouse

Scrap of pink fabric for the ear

Disk of stiff cardboard measuring 14¼ x 14¼ in. (36 x 36cm) for the backing

1 piece of fusible web measuring 2 in. (5cm) square or fabric glue

1 battery-operated clock mechanism

pair of sharp scissors

double-sided tape

contrasting colored thread for basting

coordinating colored thread for sewing

ball-headed pins

hand-sewing needle

sewing machine

Cutting out

2 cat shapes from 2 of the pieces of fabric and 4 spacer shapes from the third piece of fabric. Baste them to the cardboard shapes (see page 113).

Back a scrap of patchwork fabric, the gray and pink fabrics with fusible web following the manufacturer's instructions and cut out the mouse hole, mouse and ear.

Difficulty rating

Intermediate

Finished size

14¼ x 14¼ in. (36 x 36cm)

Sewing the cat and spacer shapes

1 Decide on the arrangement of the cat and spacer shapes (see page 114). Hand-sew two cats together, right sides together, starting with the tails. Sew the tip of one cat's tail to the tip of the other cat's tail, then work along the tails following the direction of the arrow on the illustration. Use a coordinating colored thread and a whipstitch, and finish with a double stitch (see page 114).

2 Next add a third cat, aligning the tip of the new cat's tail with the tails of the other cats, right sides together, and hand-sew this seam as before. Refer to your design arrangement for color placement. Add the fourth cat, following the direction of the arrow on the illustration and making sure the corners of each piece are aligned. Work a double stitch before you stitch the next section.

3 Hand-sew the spacers to the cats, starting at the base of the cat and working along the body following the direction of the arrow on the illustration. The patchwork panel should measure approximately 15 x 15 in. (38 x 38cm).

continued on page 26

Making the clock

4 Iron the back so that the panel lies flat. Remove the basting stitches and pieces of cardboard.

5 Decide on the position of the mouse and mouse hole and attach them to the patchwork panel using the fusible web and following the manufacturer's instructions. Repeat to add the ear.

6 Turn under the seam allowances and use short strips of double-sided tape to secure them to the back of the patchwork panel. Add extra tape in the center of the panel where the clock mechanism will go. Attach the panel to the cardboard backing. Trim any excess fabric and use the tip of a pair of scissors to make a hole in the center for the clock mechanism.

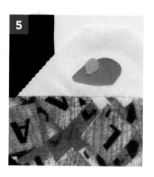

7 Attach the panel to the cardboard, making sure it is in the center of the backing. Press down firmly on the tape to make sure it is secure.

Finishing off

8 Following the manufacturer's instructions, insert the clock mechanism into the hole in the center of the mounted patchwork panel. Take care when tightening the mechanism so that you do not twist the fabric.

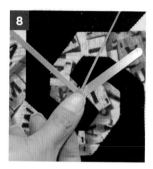

Tip

The clock can be mounted on a circular panel, as shown here, or on a square one. You can add fusible-web backed fabric numbers to the clock face if you wish. For a sturdier base, use ⅛-in. (0.3cm) MDF board and use a drill to make the hole for the mechanism. The clock mechanism will include a hook so that you can hang the clock on the wall.

Cat and Mouse Templates

Templates shown at 95%; enlarge to 100% before cutting.

For information about cutting out the template and fabric shapes, see pages 109–111.

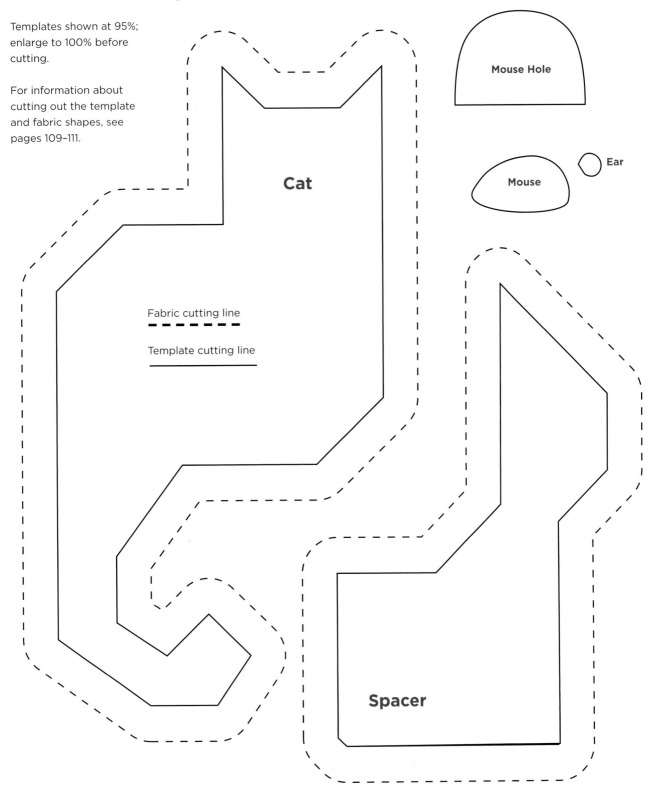

Mouse Hole

Mouse

Ear

Cat

Fabric cutting line

Template cutting line

Spacer

Farm Animals

Those familiar farmyard friends—the chicken, cow, horse and sheep—will brighten up any kitchen or nursery when their distinctive shapes are used to create an apron, tea cozy, wall hanging and child's play mat.

Chicken Apron

These happy hens look great as a pocket on this adorable apron. Using bright colors and fabrics printed with dots makes this an irresistible—and practical—addition to any kitchen.

You will need

11 Chicken Templates (see page 33) cut from thin cardboard or heavy paper stock

5 pieces of fabric measuring 14 in. (35.5cm) square for the patchwork

1 piece of fabric measuring 34 x 26 in. (86 x 66cm) for the apron

78¾-in. (2m) length of ribbon or fabric tape for the apron ties

tailor's chalk or erasable fabric pen

ruler

contrasting colored thread for basting

coordinating colored thread for sewing

safety pin

ball-headed pins

hand-sewing needle

sewing machine

Cutting out

11 chicken shapes, 2 from 4 of the pieces of fabric, and 3 from the 5th piece of fabric. Baste them to the cardboard shapes (see page 113).

Difficulty rating

Easy

Finished size

33 x 24½ in. (84 x 62.5cm)

Sewing the chicken shapes

1 Decide on the arrangement of the chicken shapes (see page 114). Hand-sew 6 chickens together in pairs, right sides together, working from the tail to the head and joining the top of one shape to the bottom of another (as shown in the illustration). Make sure the corners of each piece are aligned. Use a coordinating colored thread and a whipstitch, and finish with a double stitch (see page 114).

2 Sew an additional chicken to each pair as before, right sides together, joining the top of one shape to the bottom of another to create 3 columns of 3 chickens. Refer to your design arrangement for color placement.

3 Sew the columns together, right sides together, along the long edges as before to create a panel. Work from the bottom of the body to the top of the head of each shape. If there are any gaps, cut out sections from the 2 remaining chickens and use them to fill the spaces to make a patchwork panel measuring approximately 15¾ x 12 in. (40 x 30cm). This will be the pocket.

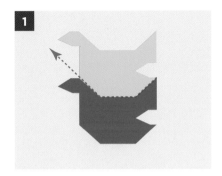

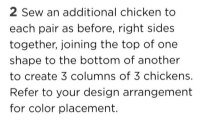

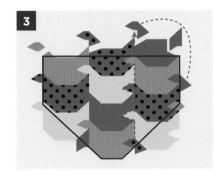

continued on page 32

Making the apron

4 Remove the basting stitches and cardboard. Press the patchwork panel on the wrong side so that all seam allowances are flat. Use a ruler and tailor's chalk or an erasable fabric pen to mark a rectangle measuring 15½ x 11¼ in. (39.4 x 28.5cm). On the bottom edge, mark the point 5 in. (13cm) in from each side. On each side, mark the point 7 in. (18cm) from the bottom. Draw a line to connect these points at each side. Trim along the marked lines. With right sides together, pin then baste a ⅜-in. (1cm) seam allowance along the side and bottom edges. Pin then baste a ⅜-in. (1cm) double-turned hem along the top edge and machine-stitch, using a coordinating colored thread. Press the seams.

5 Fold the apron fabric in half lengthwise. To create the shape of the top of the apron, mark a point 9 in. (23cm) in from one short edge, using tailor's chalk or an erasable fabric pen. Mark a second point 6 in. (15cm) in from the side edge. Use a ruler to draw a line from one point to the other, then cut away the corners.

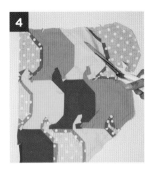

6 Unfold the apron fabric. Pin a ⅜-in. (1cm) double-turned hem along the top, bottom and sides of the apron. Do not create seams on the two slanted edges. Machine-sew the hems, using a coordinating colored thread. Press the seams.

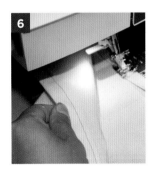

7 To create a casing for the apron ties, pin a 1-in. (2.5cm) double-turned hem along the two slanted edges. Sew the hems using a sewing machine and coordinating colored thread and keeping the stitches as close as possible to the edge. Press the seams.

8 Position the pocket on the front of the apron so it is in the center and the bottom edge is 5½ in. (14cm) from the bottom of the apron (see Assembling the Apron and Pocket on the facing page). Pin in place. Use a sewing machine and coordinating colored thread to topstitch the pocket in place along the sides and bottom (leave the top edge open). Press the seams.

9 Pin a ½–in. (1.25cm) double-turned hem on both ends of the ribbon, if using. Machine-sew in place and remove the basting stitches. Secure the safety pin to one end of the length of ribbon or tape and use it to thread the ribbon or tape through the casing on each side of the apron.

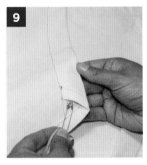

Finishing off

10 Adjust the ribbon or tape so there is a loop to go around your neck and the ties at each side are an equal length.

Chicken Template

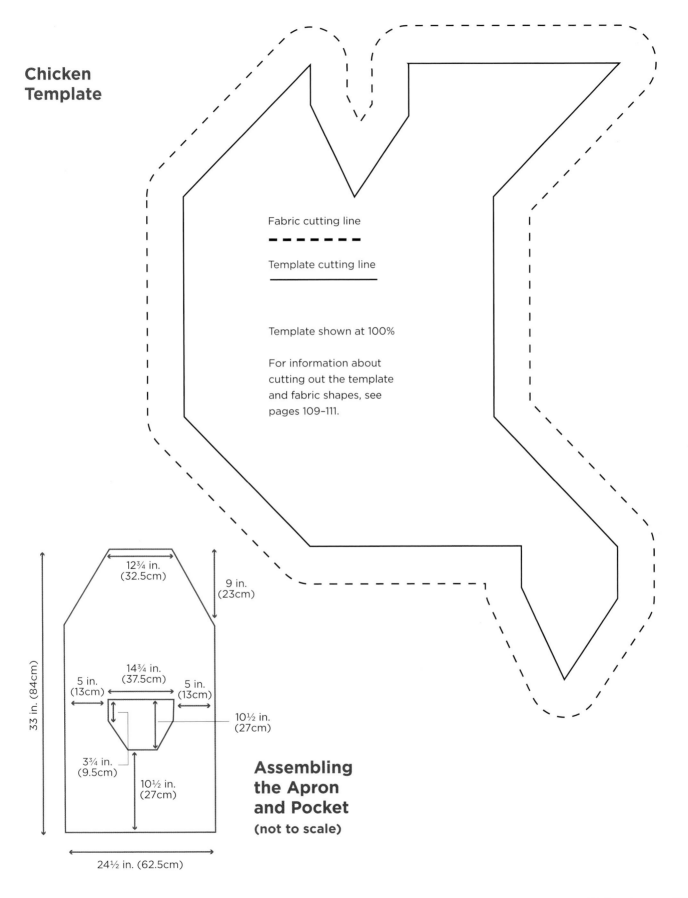

Fabric cutting line

– – – – –

Template cutting line

―――――

Template shown at 100%

For information about cutting out the template and fabric shapes, see pages 109–111.

12¾ in. (32.5cm)

9 in. (23cm)

33 in. (84cm)

14¾ in. (37.5cm)

5 in. (13cm)

5 in. (13cm)

10½ in. (27cm)

3¾ in. (9.5cm)

10½ in. (27cm)

24½ in. (62.5cm)

Assembling the Apron and Pocket
(not to scale)

Sheep Play Mat

This fluffy flock of fleecy sheep is ready to play. And what a surprise—one of them wants to stand out from the crowd!

You will need

14 Sheep Templates (see page 37) cut from thin cardboard or heavy paper stock

1 piece of white fleece fabric measuring 60 x 20 in. (150 x 50cm) for the patchwork

1 piece of black fleece fabric measuring 30 x 10 in. (76 x 25cm) for the patchwork and faces

1 piece of gray fleece fabric measuring 32 x 34 in. (81 x 86cm) for the backing and one gray face

tailor's chalk or erasable fabric pen

ruler

contrasting colored thread for basting

coordinating colored thread for sewing

ball-headed pins

hand-sewing needle

sewing machine

Cutting out

14 sheep shapes, 13 from white fleece and 1 from black fleece. Baste them to the cardboard shapes (see page 113).

One 32 x 30 in. (81 x 76cm) rectangle from the gray fleece for the backing.

13 sheep faces from the black fleece.

1 sheep face from the gray fleece.

Difficulty rating

Intermediate

Finished size

26 x 28¼ in. (66 x 72cm)

Sewing the sheep shapes

1 Decide on the arrangement of the sheep shapes (see page 114). Hand-sew the sheep together in pairs, right sides together, starting with the sides and shoulders. Sew from the bottom to the top following the direction of the arrow on the illustration. Use a coordinating colored thread and a whipstitch, and finish with a double stitch (see page 114).

2 Next align 2 pairs with right sides together, and hand-sew this seam as before. Continue to hand-sew pairs together until you have 6 pairs and 2 single sheep. Follow the direction of the arrow on the illustration and make sure the corners of each piece are aligned. Work a double stitch before you stitch the next section.

3 Hand-sew the pairs together to create 2 blocks of 6 sheep. Refer to your design arrangement for color placement. Whipstitch along the top of one block and the bottom of the other with right sides together. Add 1 single sheep on each side as shown in the illustration. You should have a panel measuring approximately 32 x 29 in. (81 x 73.6cm).

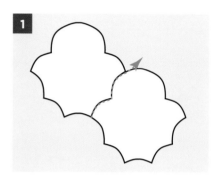

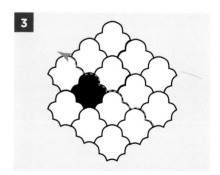

continued on page 36

Making the play mat

4 Clip the seam allowances. Remove the basting stitches and pieces of cardboard. Press the seams open on the wrong side.

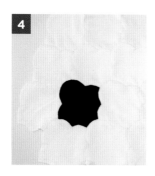

5 Position the black faces on the white sheep and the gray face on the black sheep. Pin then use a sewing machine and coordinating colored thread to topstitch them in place, sewing around the face but leaving the ears unstitched.

6 Place the backing fabric on a work surface with the wrong side facing up. Place the patchwork panel on top with the right side facing up and use tailor's chalk or an erasable fabric pen to mark around the edge of the patchwork panel so the outline is on the backing fabric. Be sure to include the seam allowance from the unstitched edges of the sheep. Remove the patchwork panel. Cut out the backing fabric along the marked lines.

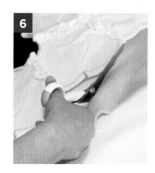

7 With right sides together, pin then baste the patchwork panel and backing fabric together. Use a sewing machine to stitch them together, leaving a ⅜-in. (1cm) seam allowance and a 3-in. (7.5cm) gap fur turning the mat right side out. Clip the seam allowances of the backing fabric to mirror the patchwork panel.

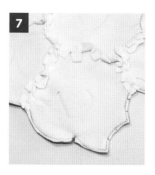

Finishing off

8 Turn the play mat right side out. Tuck in the raw edges of the gap, and use a ladder stitch and coordinating colored thread to close the gap. Press the seams on the wrong side.

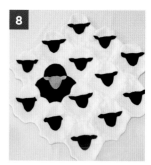

Sheep Templates

Templates shown at 100%

For information about cutting out the template and fabric shapes, see pages 109–111.

Fabric cutting line

- - - - - - -

Template cutting line

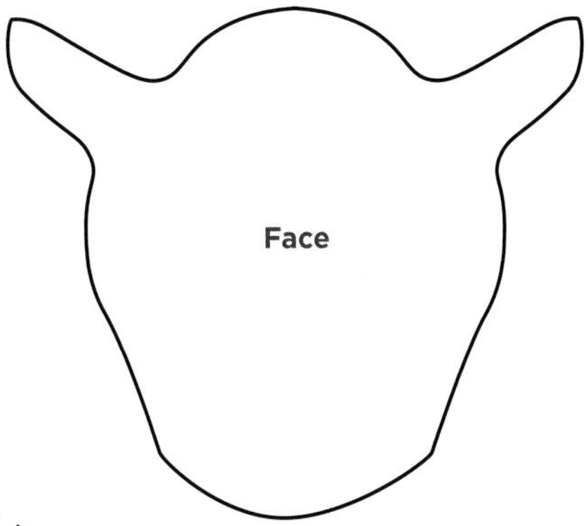

_____

Face

Cow Tea Cozy

This cozy will keep your teapot toasty and warm while you sew to your heart's content. The patchwork panel is stitched to a backing fabric to stabilize it, while a layer of batting keeps the heat in.

You will need

12 Cow Templates (see page 41) cut from thin cardboard or heavy paper stock

3 pieces of fabric measuring 16 x 16 in. (40.5 x 40.5cm) for the patchwork

2 pieces of fabric measuring 10 x 14 in. (25 x 35.5cm) for the lining

2 pieces of fabric measuring 4 x 14 in. (10 x 35.5cm) for the backing

1 piece of pink fabric measuring 5 in. (13cm) square for the noses

1 piece of black fabric measuring 5 in. (13cm) square for the eyes and nostrils

1 piece of batting measuring 19 x 13¾ in. (48.2 x 35.5cm)

fusible web

tailor's chalk or erasable fabric pen

ruler

contrasting colored thread for basting

coordinating colored thread for sewing

ball-headed pins

hand-sewing needle

sewing machine

Cutting out

12 cow shapes, 4 from each of the patchwork fabrics (see page 109). Baste them to the cardboard shapes (see page 113).

Back the pink and black fabrics with fusible web following the manufacturer's instructions. Cut out 4 noses from the pink fabric and 12 pairs of eyelashes and nostrils from the black.

Difficulty rating

Intermediate

Finished size

12¾ x 9¼ in. (32.5 x 23.5cm)

Sewing the cow shapes

1 Decide on the arrangement of the cow shapes (see page 114). Hand-sew two cows together, right sides together, at the horns, following the direction of the arrow on the illustration. Use a coordinating colored thread and a whipstitch, and finish with a double stitch (see page 114). Add a third cow to make a row of 3 cows joined at the horns. Repeat to make 4 rows of 3 cows.

2 Assemble 2 rows of cows so that the jaws interlock. Refer to your design arrangement for color placement. With right sides together, hand-sew the rows together as before, following the direction of the arrow on the illustration. Repeat with the 2 remaining rows of cows.

3 Assemble the 2 patchwork sections so that the ears and horns interlock. With right sides together, hand-sew the panels together as before, following the direction of the arrow on the illustration. You will have a panel that is 3 cows wide by 4 cows tall. You should have a panel measuring approximately 26 x 13 in. (66 x 33cm). Iron the back so that the panel lies flat.

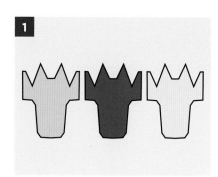

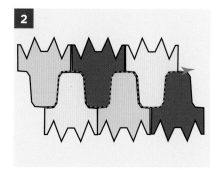

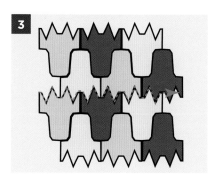

continued on page 40

Making the tea cozy

4 Following the manufacturer's instructions, use the fusible web to attach the eyelashes, using the template on the facing page as a reference. Repeat to attach noses to 4 of the cows and nostrils to all the cows. Remove the basting stitches and cardboard. Press the seams open on the wrong side.

5 Use a sewing machine and a coordinating colored thread to topstitch the noses.

6 Place the patchwork panel right side up on a work surface and use a ruler and tailor's chalk or an erasable fabric pen to mark a straight edge on each short side so that the panel is 13¾ in. (35cm) wide. Trim the panel along the marked lines. Position a strip of backing fabric behind each long edge of the panel, aligning the sides so that the panel measures 19¼ x 13¾ in. (48.9 x 35cm); pin into position. Use a sewing machine and a contrasting colored thread to topstitch the edges of the patchwork panel to attach it to the backing fabric ¼ in. (0.5cm) from the edge.

7 Position the batting against the wrong side of the patchwork panel and pin in place. Fold in half widthwise with the batting on the outside. Pin the sides, then use a sewing machine and a coordinating colored thread to sew them together, leaving a ½-in. (1.25 cm) seam allowance. Turn right side out. Position the pieces of lining fabric with right sides together. Pin both short edges, and one-quarter of the way along both sides of one long edge. Use a sewing machine and a coordinating colored thread to sew them together, leaving a ½-in. (1.25 cm) seam allowance. Do not turn right side out.

8 Place the patchwork inside the lining on the open long edge, aligning the side seams. Pin the layers together along the long edges. Use a sewing machine and a coordinating colored thread to sew them together, leaving a ½-in. (1.25 cm) seam allowance.

9 Turn the cozy right side out through the gap in the lining. Tuck in the raw edges of the lining and use a ladder stitch to sew the gap closed. Press the fabric.

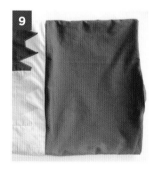

Finishing off

10 Push the lining into the tea cozy until smooth. Use a sewing machine and coordinating colored thread to topstitch around the base ¼ in. (0.5cm) from the edge (see page 117).

Cow Templates

Templates shown at 85%; enlarge to 100% before cutting.

For information about cutting out the template and fabric shapes, see pages 109–111.

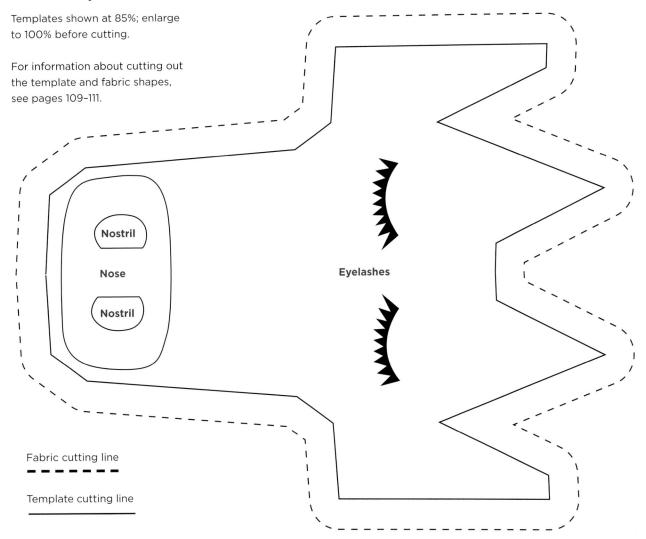

Nostril

Nose

Nostril

Eyelashes

Fabric cutting line

Template cutting line

Horse Wall Hanging

This monochromatic wall hanging features a stable of majestic horses. A pair of fabric tabs suspends the panel from a pole.

You will need

16 Horse Templates (see page 45) cut from thin cardboard or heavy paper stock

1 piece of black fabric measuring 40 in. (100cm) square for the patchwork, backing and tabs

1 piece of white fabric measuring 40 x 12 in. (100 x 30cm) for the patchwork

¾-in. (2cm) diameter metal pole or wooden dowel, 20 in. (50cm) long

tailor's chalk or erasable fabric pen

ruler

contrasting colored thread for basting

coordinating colored thread for sewing

ball-headed pins

hand-sewing needle

sewing machine

Cutting out

16 horse shapes, 8 from each fabric. Baste them to the cardboard shapes (see page 113).

One 32 x 22½-in. (81 x 57cm) rectangle from the black fabric.

Four 4 x 6-in. (10 x 15cm) rectangles for the tabs from the black fabric.

Difficulty rating

Intermediate

Finished size

29½ x 20¼ in. (75 x 51.5cm) at longest and widest points, excluding the tabs

Sewing the horse shapes

1 Decide on the arrangement of the horse shapes (see page 114). Hand-sew the horses together in pairs, right sides together, starting with the faces. Sew the bottom of the neck of 1 horse to the top of the head of the other horse, following the direction of the arrow on the illustration. Use a coordinating colored thread and a whipstitch, and finish with a double stitch (see page 114).

2 Next align 2 pairs of horses with the heads back to back, right sides together, and hand-sew this seam as before. Follow the direction of the arrow on the illustration and make sure the corners of each piece are aligned. Work a double stitch before you stitch the next section. Repeat to make 3 rows of 4 horses. Add a third pair of horses to 2 of the rows. You will have 2 rows of 6 horses and 1 row of 4.

3 Hand-sew the rows together. Whipstitch along the tops of the heads with right sides together. You should have a diamond-shaped panel measuring approximately 33 x 23 in. (84 x 58.5cm).

continued on page 44

Making the wall hanging

4 Clip the seam allowances. Remove the basting stitches and pieces of cardboard. Press the seams flat on the wrong side.

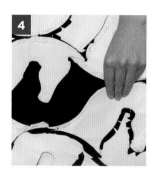

5 To make the tabs, pin 2 fabric rectangles together with right sides facing. Use a sewing machine to stitch along both long edges, leaving a ¼-in. (0.5cm) seam allowance. Turn right side out and press flat. Repeat to make a second tab.

6 Place the backing fabric on a work surface with the wrong side facing up. Place the patchwork panel on top with the right side facing up, and use tailor's chalk or an erasable fabric pen to mark around the edge of the patchwork panel so the outline is on the backing fabric. Be sure to include the seam allowance from the unstitched edges of the horses. Remove the patchwork panel. Cut out the backing fabric along the marked lines.

Tip

When determining the position of the tabs, pin them in place and then hang the panel to make sure it hangs evenly and the tabs are centered on the patchwork design.

7 With right sides together, pin the patchwork panel and backing fabric together. Use a sewing machine to stitch them together along the sides, leaving a ⅜-in. (1cm) seam allowance. Determine the position of the tabs, making sure they are an equal distance from each side, and trim the fabric so there is a straight edge where they will be attached. Do not turn the wall hanging right side out.

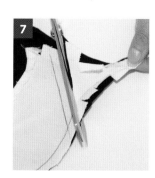

8 Fold the tabs in half widthwise and position them between the patchwork and backing fabric on the unsewn edge, aligning the raw edges, and pin. Check their position (see Tip). Machine-sew in place, leaving a gap between the tabs.

9 Turn the wall hanging right side out through the gap and pin then baste the remaining seam closed. Hand-stitch the seam using a whipstitch and a coordinating colored thread (a contrasting colored thread has been used in the photograph to show the stitches).

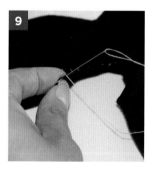

Finishing off

10 Press the wall hanging on the wrong side and insert the dowel into the tabs.

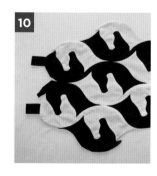

Horse Template

Template shown at 100%

For information about cutting out the template and fabric shapes, see pages 109–111.

Fabric cutting line

- - - - - - - -

Template cutting line

_____

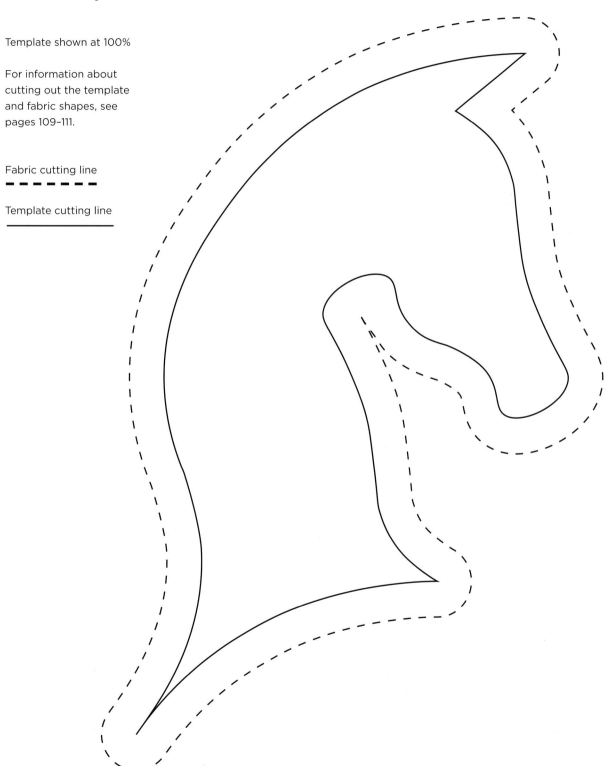

Water Creatures

Whether they're swimming in the ocean or scampering at the water's edge, these goldfish, angelfish, turtles and penguins create splashes of water all around them. Bring them into your home by making a stool cover, pillow, brush roll and journal cover.

Angelfish Brush Roll

This practical project will keep your make-up brushes in perfect order. I've chosen batik fabrics to add to the watery effect, but alternatively you can embellish plain fabrics with embroidery for added visual appeal.

You will need

12 Angelfish Templates (see page 51) cut from thin cardboard or heavy paper stock

2 pieces of fabric measuring 18 x 12 in. (45 x 30cm) for the patchwork

1 piece of fabric measuring 12½ x 6 in. (32 x 15cm) for the pockets

1 piece of fabric measuring 13¼ x 9¼ in. (33.5 x 23.5cm) for the backing

1 piece of batting measuring 13¼ x 9¼ in. (33.5 x 23.5cm)

20-in. (50cm) length of ribbon

tailor's chalk or erasable fabric pen

ruler

ball-headed pins

contrasting colored thread for basting

coordinating colored thread for sewing

hand-sewing needle

sewing machine

Cutting out

12 fish shapes, 6 from each of the 2 pieces of fabric. Baste them to the cardboard shapes (see page 113).

Difficulty rating

Intermediate

Finished size

12½ x 8½ in. (32 x 21.5cm)

Sewing the fish shapes

1 Decide on the arrangement of the fish shapes (see page 114). Hand-sew 2 fish cut from each fabric together in pairs, right sides together. Start by joining a nose and tail and stitch along the fins and the bottom of the body (as shown in the illustration). Sew one straight seam at a time, making sure the corners of each piece are aligned and working a double stitch before you change direction. Use a coordinating colored thread and a whipstitch, and finish with a double stitch (see page 114).

2 Hand-sew pairs of fish together as before, joining them at the tails, to create 3 sets of 4 fish.

3 Sew the 3 sets of fish together, joining the top edges of the bodies together, to create a patchwork panel measuring approximately 13¼ x 9¼ in. (33.5 x 23.5cm).

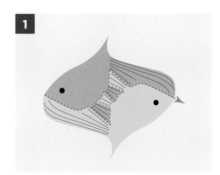

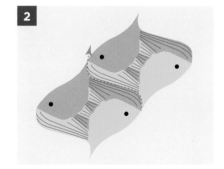

continued on page 50

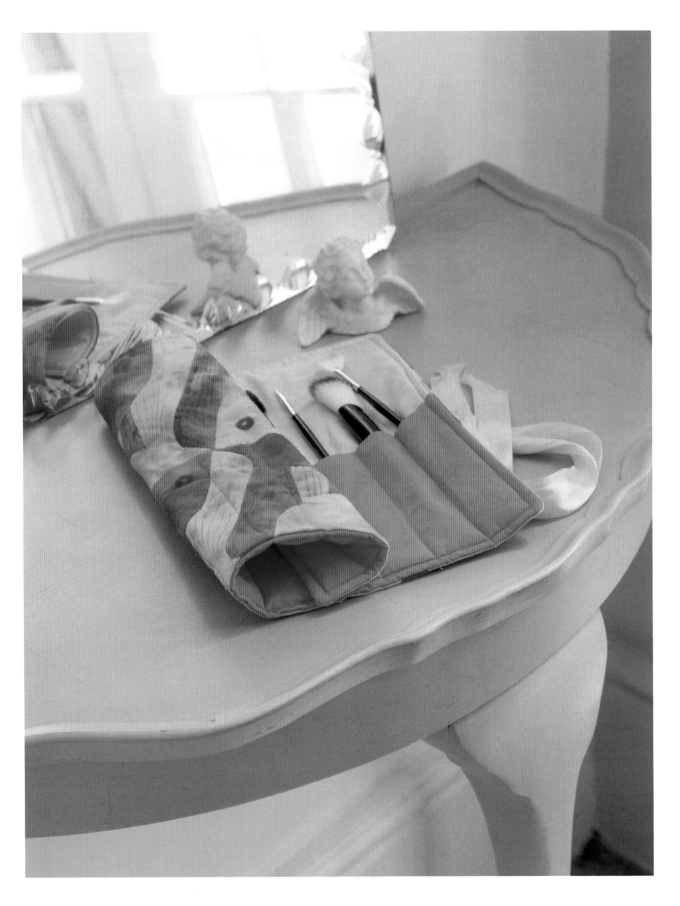

Making the roll

4 Remove the basting stitches and pieces of cardboard. Press the patchwork panel on the wrong side. Use a ruler and tailor's chalk or an erasable fabric pen to mark a 13¼ x 9¼-in. (33.5 x 23.5cm) rectangle in the center of the panel. Trim along the marked lines.

5 On the front of the patchwork panel, use a pin to mark a point in the center 2 in. (5cm) from one short edge. Fold the length of ribbon in half and pin the fold at the marked point. Use a sewing machine and coordinating colored thread to attach the ribbon.

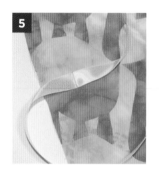

6 Pin a ⅜-in. (1cm) double-turned hem along one long edge of the pocket fabric (see page 120). Machine-sew the hem using a coordinating colored thread.

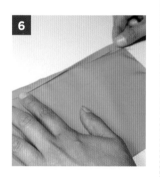

7 Place the batting on a work surface. Place the backing fabric on top, right side up, then add the pocket fabric, right side up and with the raw edges aligned. Place the patchwork panel on top (right side facing down). Pin the edges.

8 Sew around the edges, leaving a ⅜-in. (1cm) seam allowance and a 3-in. (7.5cm) gap in the bottom edge. Take care not to catch the ends of the ribbon in the stitching. Trim the seam allowance to ¼ in. (0.5cm), and cut the corners at an angle so that they will not be bulky.

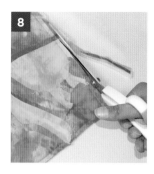

9 Turn the panel right side out through the gap. Tuck in the raw edges and baste the gap closed. Press the fabric. Use a sewing machine and coordinating colored thread to topstitch around the panel ¼ in. (0.5cm) from the edge (see page 117).

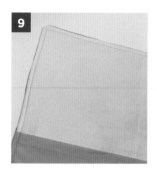

Finishing off

10 Use a ruler and tailor's chalk or an erasable fabric pen to mark the position of the pocket dividers—about 1¼ in. (3cm) apart—then stitch using a sewing machine and coordinating colored thread. Roll up the brush roll and tie the ribbon in a bow to secure it.

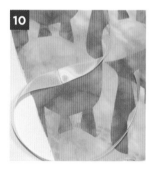

Angelfish Template

Template shown at 100%

For information about cutting out the template and fabric shapes, see pages 109–111.

Fabric cutting line

- - - - - - -

Template cutting line

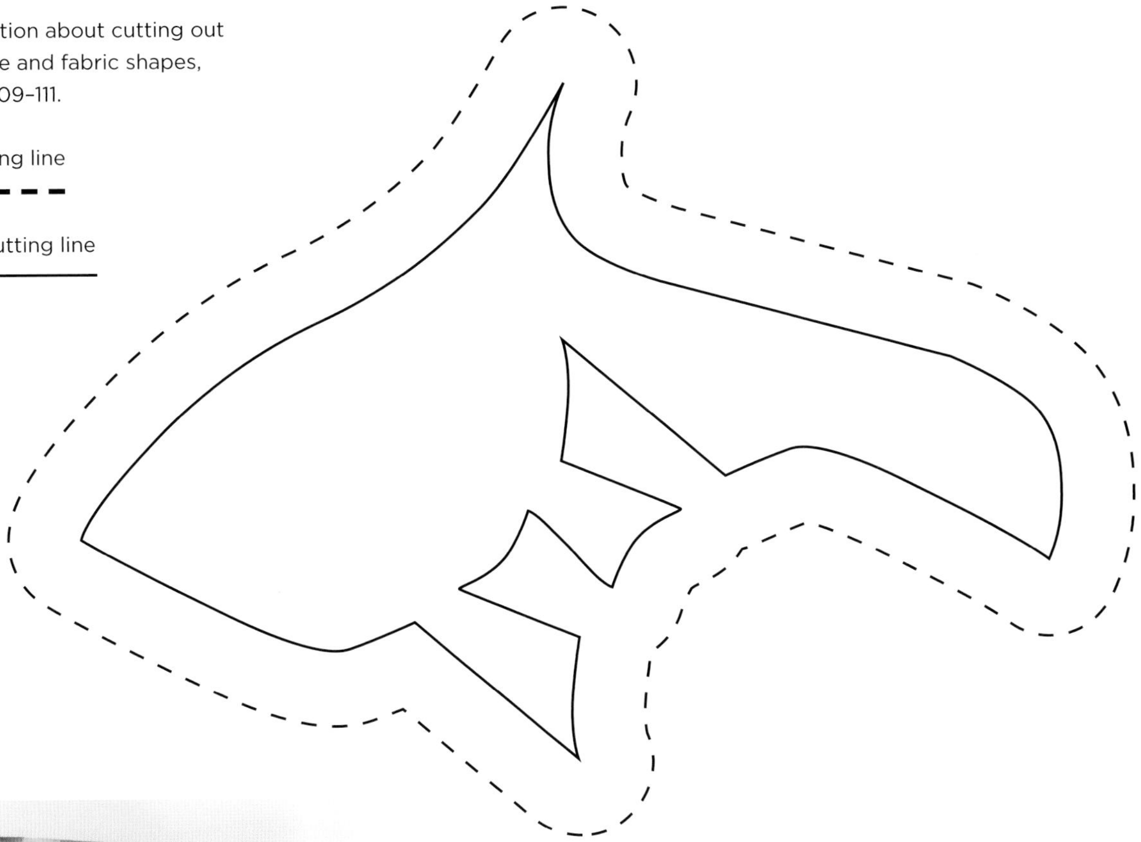

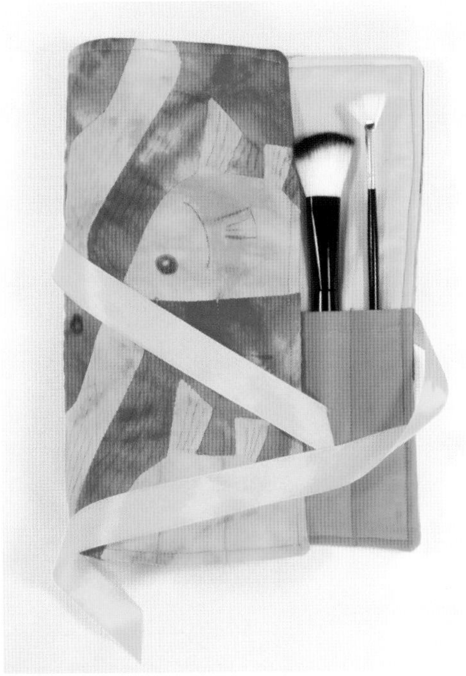

_____

Tip

You can add details to your brush roll by using a fabric marker to draw eyes on the fish and embellish the tails and fins. Alternatively, you can embroider these details.

Turtle Stool Cover

Add a splash of color to a stool by covering the seat with a herd of colorful turtles. Once you have joined the turtles and their shells together, the square, box form of this cover is easy to assemble.

You will need

16 Turtle Templates (see page 55) cut from thin cardboard or heavy paper stock

4 pieces of fabric measuring 12 in. (30cm) square for the patchwork

4 pieces of fabric measuring 14 x 8½ in. (35.5 x 21.5cm) for the sides of the stool cover

4 pieces of fleece fabric measuring 6 in. (15cm) square for the turtle shells

tailor's chalk or erasable fabric pen

ruler

contrasting colored thread for basting

coordinating colored thread for sewing

ball-headed pins

hand-sewing needle

sewing machine

Cutting out

16 turtle shapes, 4 from each of the fabrics. Baste them to the cardboard shapes (see page 113).

16 turtle shells, 4 from each color of fleece.

Difficulty rating

Intermediate

Finished size

13½ in. (34.5cm) square

Sewing the turtle shapes

1 Decide on the arrangement of the turtle shapes (see page 114). Hand-sew the turtles together in pairs, right sides together, starting with the heads. Sew the top of one head to the tail of the other turtle following the direction of the arrow on the illustration. Use a coordinating colored thread and a whipstitch, and finish with a double stitch (see page 114). Then sew the top of one flipper to the side of the other as before.

2 Next align the head corner of one turtle with the head of another turtle, right sides together, and hand-sew this seam as before. Continue to hand-sew pairs together, following the direction of the arrow on the illustration and making sure the corners of each piece are aligned. Work a double stitch before you stitch the next section.

3 When you have sewn the 16 turtles together in sets of 4, hand-sew the sets together to create a panel about 14 in. (35.5cm) square. Refer to your design arrangement for color placement. Whipstitch along the sides with right sides together. Iron the back so that the panel lies flat.

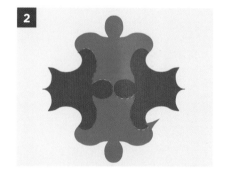

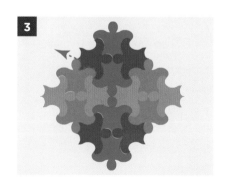

continued on page 54

Making the cover

4 Decide on the arrangement of the turtle shells. Pin them in position in the center of the turtles' backs. Use a sewing machine and coordinating colored thread to topstitch around the edge of each shell ¼ in. (0.5cm) from the edge (see page 117). Place the patchwork panel right side up on a work surface and use a ruler and tailor's chalk or an erasable fabric pen to mark a 15-in. (38cm) square in the center of the panel. Trim the panel along the marked lines. Remove the basting stitches and cardboard. Press the seams open on the wrong side.

Tip

Instead of using a sewing machine straight stitch to attach the shells, you can use a decorative zigzag stitch. Alternatively, hand-sew them using a backstitch (see page 123) and contrasting embroidery floss.

5 Place the patchwork panel and one of the pieces of fabric for the side of the stool cover together, with right sides facing and so that one edge of the panel and one long edge of the side fabric are aligned; pin. Repeat with the remaining side pieces; they should overlap by ¼ in. (0.5cm) to allow them to be joined later. Use a sewing machine to stitch around all four sides of the patchwork panel, leaving a ¾-in. (2cm) seam allowance. Sew with the right side of the panel facing you, to allow you to keep the patchwork seams open. Trim the seam allowance to ⅜ in. (1cm).

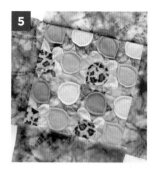

6 Pin, then baste the sides of the stool cover together. Use a sewing machine to stitch around all four sides, leaving a ¼-in. (0.5cm) seam allowance.

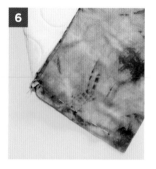

Finishing off

7 Use a sewing machine to stitch a double-turned hem (see page 120) along the bottom edge of the side pieces, using a ½-in. (1.25cm) seam allowance.

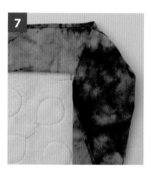

Turtle Templates

Templates shown at 100%

For information about cutting out the template and fabric shapes, see pages 109–111.

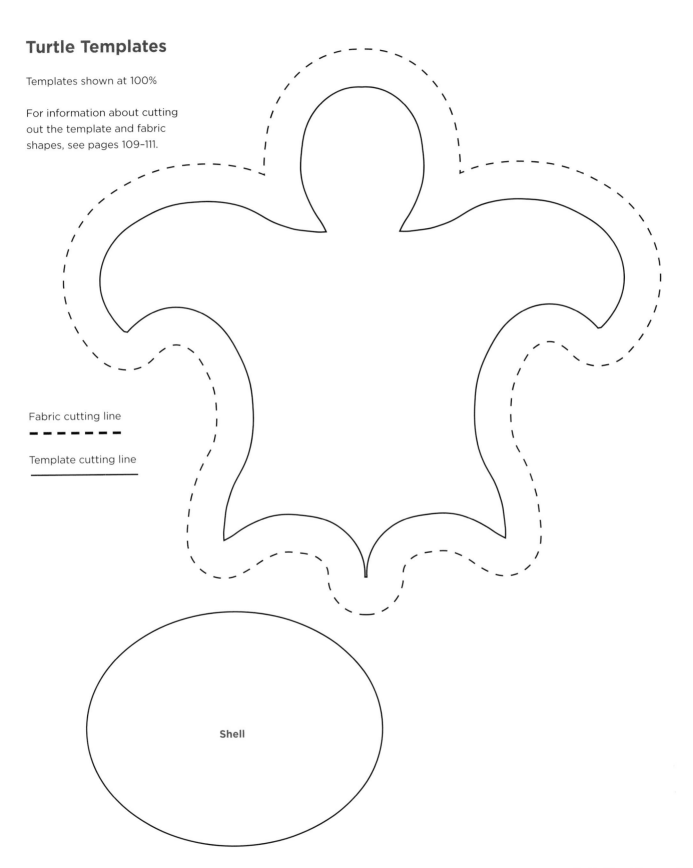

Fabric cutting line

Template cutting line

Shell

Goldfish Journal Cover

Jotting down notes in your journal will be a pleasure when it is protected by this goldfish cover. I combined plain blue fabrics for the water with fabric printed with fish shapes which I fussy-cut to make this fabulous fishy project.

You will need

10 Goldfish Templates (see page 59) cut from thin cardboard or heavy paper stock

3 pieces of fabric measuring 24 x 13 in. (61 x 33cm) for the patchwork

1 piece of fabric measuring 2 x 9 in. (5 x 23cm) for the spine

2 pieces of fabric measuring 9 x 5 in. (23 x 13cm) for the cover flaps

1 piece of fabric measuring 13 x 9 in. (33 x 23cm) for the inside front flap pocket

1 piece of fabric measuring 13 x 9 in. (33 x 23cm) for the lining

A5 hardback notebook

tailor's chalk or erasable fabric pen

ruler

contrasting colored thread for basting

coordinating colored thread for sewing

ball-headed pins

hand-sewing needle

sewing machine

Cutting out

10 goldfish shapes, 3 each from 2 of the patchwork fabrics and 4 from the third patchwork fabric. Baste them to the cardboard shapes (see page 113).

Difficulty rating

Easy

Finished size

12½ x 8½ in. (32 x 21.5cm)

Sewing the goldfish shapes

1 Decide on the arrangement of the fish shapes (see page 114). Hand-sew 2 goldfish together in pairs, right sides together. Start by joining a nose and tail and stitch along the sides of the body (as shown in the illustration). Use a coordinating colored thread and a whipstitch and finish with a double stitch (see page 114). Continue to hand-sew pairs together, following the direction of the arrow on the illustration.

2 Sew the pairs of fish together to make 2 columns of 4 fish using the same technique. Refer to your design arrangement for color placement. Sew a fifth fish to each of the columns as before to make 2 patchwork panels of 5 fish. Each panel should measure approximately 16 x 9 in. (40.5 x 23cm).

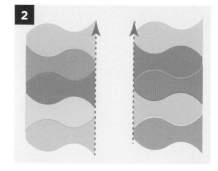

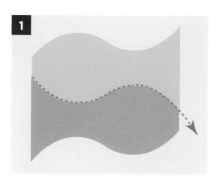

continued on page 58

Making the journal cover

3 Remove the basting stitches and cardboard. Press the panel so the seam allowances are flat. Pin the panels to the spine, right sides together. Machine-sew, using coordinating colored thread and a ⅜-in. (1cm) seam allowance.

4 Use a ruler and tailor's chalk or an erasable fabric pen to draw a straight line across the top and bottom of the patchwork-spine panel so the edges are aligned with the ends of the spine fabric. Trim the fabric along the marked lines. The panel should measure approximately 13 x 9 in. (33 x 23cm).

5 Fold and pin a ⅜-in. (1cm) double-turned hem along one long edge of both pieces of fabric for the cover flaps (see page 120). Machine-sew the hem using coordinating colored thread. Press on the wrong side.

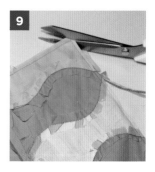

6 To make the inside front flap pocket, fold and then press a ⅜-in. (1cm) seam allowance along each edge. Topstitch one short edge—this will be the top of the pocket.

7 Position the pocket on the front cover flap in the center of the width and 5 in. (13cm) from the bottom, with the right sides of both pieces facing up. Pin then topstitch in place along the sides and bottom of the pocket.

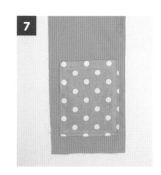

8 Place the lining fabric on a work surface with the right side facing up. Position a cover flap on each side, with right sides facing up and raw edges aligned. Finally, put the patchwork fabric on top, with the wrong side facing up. Pin the edges. Machine-sew around the edges, using coordinating colored thread and leaving a ⅜-in. (1cm) seam allowance and a 3-in. (7.5cm) gap in the bottom edge.

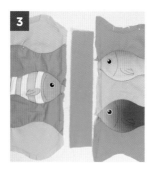

9 Trim the seam allowance to ¼ in. (0.5cm) and cut the corners at an angle so they will not be bulky. Turn the cover right side out through the gap. Tuck in the raw edges and whipstitch the gap closed, using coordinating colored thread.

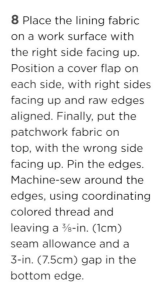

Finishing off

10 Press the journal cover and insert the book covers into the fabric flaps.

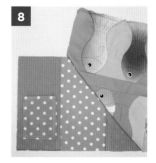

Goldfish Template

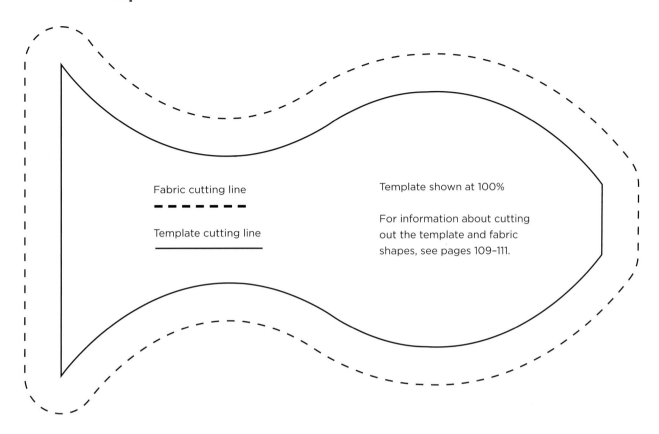

Fabric cutting line

– – – – – – –

Template cutting line

───────────

Template shown at 100%

For information about cutting out the template and fabric shapes, see pages 109–111.

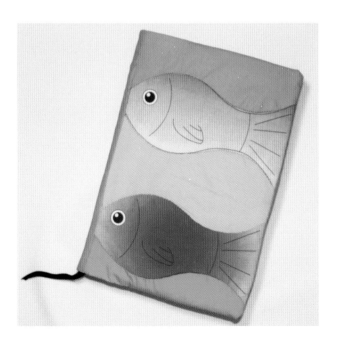

Tip

If you cannot find a suitable fish fabric, cut the fish from plain fabric and embellish them with embroidery.

Penguin Hot Pad

Keep your cool in the kitchen with the help of this waddle of penguins, which hides a cute baby bird in the center. The hot pad will protect your hands from anything that's too hot and bring a smile to mealtimes.

You will need

7 Penguin Templates (see page 63) cut from thin cardboard or heavy paper stock

2 pieces of black fabric measuring 19 in. (48.2cm) square for the patchwork and backing

1 piece of gray fabric measuring 7 in. (18cm) square for the patchwork

1 piece of white fabric and 1 piece of orange fabric, each measuring 6 x 12 in. (12 x 30cm) for the appliqué

1 piece of foil-backed batting measuring 19 in. (48.2cm) square

1 piece of fusible web measuring 12 in. (30cm) square

black fabric marking pen

ruler

tailor's chalk or erasable fabric pen

contrasting colored thread for basting

coordinating colored thread for sewing

ball-headed pins

hand-sewing needle

sewing machine

Cutting out

6 penguin shapes, 1 from gray and 5 from black. Baste them to the cardboard shapes (see page 113).

Back the white, orange and remaining black fabrics with fusible web following the manufacturer's instructions. Cut out 12 adult eyes, 2 baby eyes and 6 tummies from white; 12 feet and 6 beaks from orange; and 1 baby penguin head and beak, and 2 feet from black.

Difficulty rating

Easy

Finished size

15 in. (38cm) square

Sewing the penguin shapes

1 Decide on the arrangement of the penguin shapes (see page 114). Hand-sew the bottom left side of the baby penguin to the top right side of an adult penguin, right sides together. Sew from the base to the top, following the direction of the arrow on the illustration. Use a coordinating colored thread and a whipstitch, and finish with a double stitch (see page 114).

2 Continue to add adult penguins around the baby penguin. Follow the direction of the arrow on the illustration and make sure the corners of each piece are aligned. Work a double stitch before you stitch the next section. You should have a panel approximately 19 in. (48.2cm) square. Remove all the basting stitches and cardboard. Press the seams open on the wrong side.

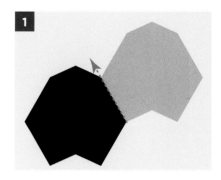

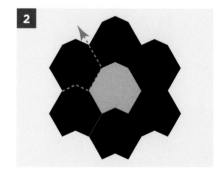

continued on page 62

Making the hot pad

3 Using the template on the facing page for reference, position the tummies, feet, eyes and beaks on the adult penguins and iron into place, following the manufacturer's instructions.

4 Position the baby penguin's head, beak and feet as shown and then iron into place, following the manufacturer's instructions.

5 Use a fabric marking pen to draw the pupils onto the eyes.

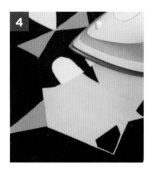

6 Place the backing fabric on a work surface with the wrong side facing up. Place the patchwork panel on top with the right side facing up. Use tailor's chalk or an erasable fabric pen to mark around the edge of the panel, including a ⅜-in. (1cm) seam allowance. Cut out the backing fabric along the marked lines. Repeat to cut out the batting. Place the penguin panel on a work surface, right side up. Place the batting on top, followed by the backing fabric, with the right side facing down. Align the edges. Pin the layers together. Machine-sew around the edges, leaving a ⅜-in. (1cm) seam allowance and a 3-in. (7.5cm) gap in one edge.

Finishing Off

7 Trim the excess batting and snip in to the internal corners so they will not be bulky. Turn the project right sides out through the gap. Tuck in the raw edges and use a ladder stitch (see page 121) and a coordinating thread to sew the gap closed. Press the seams flat.

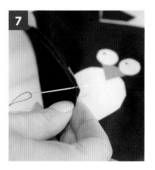

Penguin Templates

Templates shown at 70%; enlarge to 100% before cutting out.

For information about cutting out the template and fabric shapes, see pages 109–111.

Fabric cutting line

Template cutting line

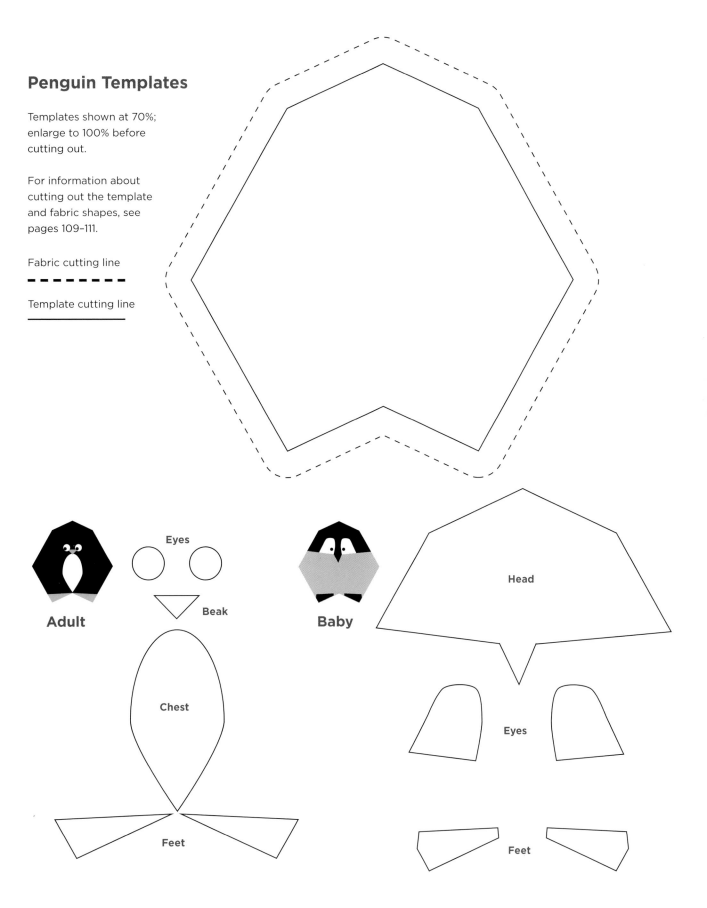

Adult

Eyes

Beak

Chest

Feet

Baby

Head

Eyes

Feet

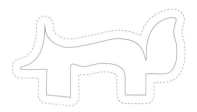

Forest Animals

Deep in the undergrowth or high up in the branches of a tree, the hedgehog, fox, bear and owl enjoy the fresh air of the forest. Store your knitting in a project bag, make a case for your laptop, and create a seat pad or baby's blanket featuring these country critters.

Owl Portfolio

These wise owls will look after your documents for you! Simply slip your papers inside this portfolio and snap closed.

You will need

9 Owl Templates (see page 69) cut from thin cardboard or heavy paper stock

9 pieces of fabric measuring 5 x 5 in. (13 x 13cm) for the patchwork

1 piece of fabric measuring 13 x 37½ in. (33 x 95.2cm) for the outside of the portfolio

1 piece of fabric measuring 13 x 37½ in. (33 x 95.2cm) for the portfolio lining

scraps of felt or fleece fabrics for the chests and beaks

scraps of fabric for the wings

9 pairs of buttons for the eyes

press stud fastener

tailor's chalk or erasable fabric pen

ruler

contrasting colored thread for basting

coordinating colored thread for sewing

black embroidery floss

ball-headed pins

hand-sewing needle

sewing machine

Cutting Out

9 owl shapes, 1 from each fabric. Baste them to the cardboard shapes (see page 113).

9 beaks and chests from the scraps of felt or fleece.

36 wings from the scraps of fabric (4 for each owl).

Difficulty rating

Intermediate

Finished size

12 x 16½ in. (30 x 42cm)

Sewing the owl shapes

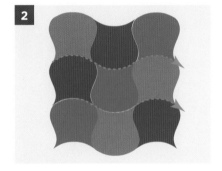

1 Decide on the arrangement of the owl shapes (see page 114). Hand-sew the owls together in pairs, right sides together, starting at the tip of one ear. Sew from the top to the bottom of the sides following the direction of the arrow on the illustration. Use a coordinating colored thread and a whipstitch, and finish with a double stitch (see page 114). Add a third owl in the same way. Repeat until you have 3 rows of 3 owls.

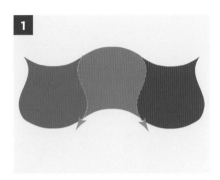

2 When you have sewn the 9 owls together in rows of 3, hand-sew the rows together. Refer to your design arrangement for color placement. Whipstitch along the base of 1 row and the top of another with right sides together. Remove the basting stitches and pieces of cardboard. Press the seams open on the wrong side. You should have a panel measuring approximately 11 x 15 in. (28 x 38cm).

continued on page 68

Making the portfolio

3 Place the fabric for the outside of the portfolio on a work surface with the right side facing down. Use a ruler and tailor's chalk or an erasable fabric pen to mark a line 3½ in. (9cm) from one end. This will be the flap. Mark a second line 17 in. (43cm) from the other end. This will be the fold at the base of the portfolio. Repeat for the lining fabric.

4 Place the patchwork panel, right side up, in the center of the right side of the fabric for the outside of the portfolio. Pin in place, making sure the seam allowance is tucked under the shapes. Topstitch the panel to the fabric by machine, sewing around each owl using a contrasting colored thread and leaving a ¼-in. (0.5cm) seam allowance (see page 120). Pin a chest onto each owl, positioning it in the center of the body and ½ in. (1.25cm) from the bottom. Topstitch in position as before, aligning the top of the wings with the top of the chest.

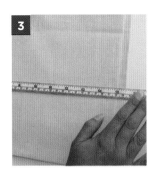

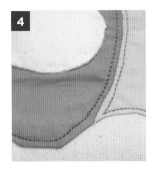

5 Place the wing shapes together in pairs (right sides together). Pin then machine-stitch around the curved edges, leaving a ¼-in. (0.5cm) seam allowance. Turn right side out and press. Fold in a ¼-in. (0.5cm) seam allowance at the top of each wing and pin to the owls. Topstitch in place as before.

6 Sew on the button eyes using black embroidery floss (see page 118). Topstitch the beaks to the owls, leaving a ¼-in. (0.5cm) seam allowance.

7 Using the line marked for the base as a guide, fold the fabric for the outside of the portfolio with right sides facing. Pin the side seams, then machine-sew the sides of the outside of the portfolio, leaving a ½-in. (1.25cm) seam allowance. Repeat for the lining, leaving a 3-in. (7.5cm) gap in one edge. Place the fabric for the outside of the portfolio (right side out) inside the fabric for the lining (inside out). Pin the seams. Machine-stitch the raw seams, leaving a ½-in. (1.25cm) seam allowance. Turn the portfolio right side out through the gap in the lining. Turn in the raw edges and use a ladder stitch to close the gap.

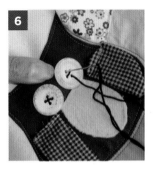

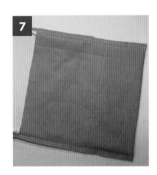

Finishing off

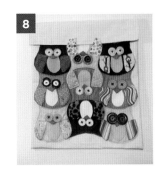

8 Topstitch the edge of the flap using a coordinating colored thread and leaving a ¼-in. (0.5cm) seam allowance. Attach the press stud to the flap.

Owl Templates

Templates shown at 70%; enlarge to 100% before cutting out.

For information about cutting out the template and fabric shapes, see pages 109–111.

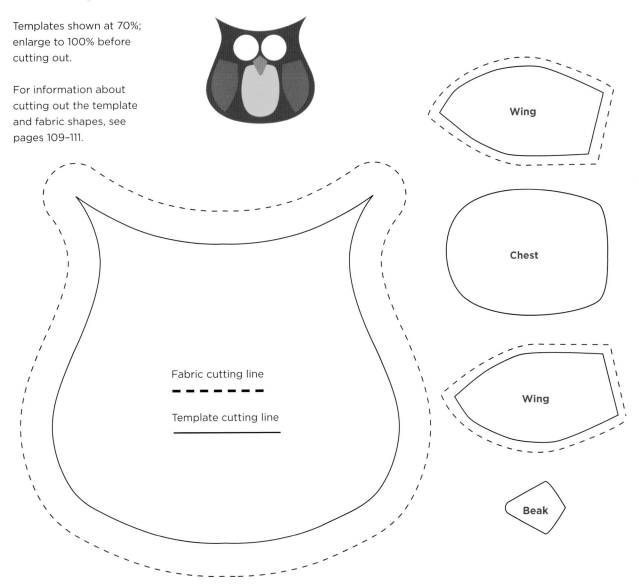

Wing

Chest

Wing

Beak

Fabric cutting line

Template cutting line

Hedgehog Project Bag

Store your knitting materials in this generously sized project bag. There's plenty of room for your needles and yarn, as well as your work in progress.

You will need

6 Hedgehog Templates (see page 73) cut from thin cardboard or heavy paper stock

6 pieces of brown fabric measuring 9 x 6 in. (23 x 15cm) for the patchwork

2 pieces of fabric measuring 9 x 17 in. (23 x 43cm) for the lining

1 piece of beige fabric measuring 8 x 12 in. (20 x 30cm) for the faces

1 piece of heavyweight calico measuring 17 in. (43cm) square for the outer fabric

1 piece of batting measuring 17 in. (43cm) square

1 piece of fusible web measuring 8 x 12 in. (20 x 30cm)

six ½-in. (1.25cm) black plastic safety eyes

12-in. (30cm) zipper

tailor's chalk or erasable fabric pen

ruler

contrasting colored thread for basting

coordinating colored thread for sewing

ball-headed pins

hand-sewing needle

sewing machine with a zipper foot

seam ripper

Cutting out

6 hedgehog shapes, 1 from each of the brown fabrics. Baste them to the cardboard shapes (see page 113).

Back the beige fabric with fusible web following the manufacturer's instructions. Cut out 6 faces.

Difficulty rating

Intermediate

Finished size

15¼ x 7¼ in. (39 x 18.5cm)

Sewing the hedgehog shapes

1 Decide on the arrangement of the hedgehog shapes (see page 114). Hand-sew 2 hedgehogs together, end to end, with right sides together. Work following the direction of the arrow on the illustration. Use a coordinating colored thread and a whipstitch, and finish with a double stitch (see page 114).

2 Next align 2 hedgehogs, nose to nose, with right sides together, and hand-sew this seam as before. Follow the direction of the arrow on the illustration and make sure the corners of each piece are aligned. Work a double stitch before you stitch the next section. Repeat with the remaining hedgehogs.

3 Hand-sew the pairs of hedgehogs together to create a panel 2 hedgehogs wide and 3 hedgehogs deep. Refer to your design arrangement for color placement. Whipstitch along the tops and bottoms of the shapes, with right sides together, to create a rectangle. You should have a rectangle measuring approximately 13 x 6 in. (33 x 15cm). Remove all of the basting stitches and cardboard. Iron the seams flat on the wrong side.

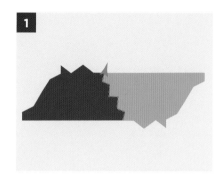

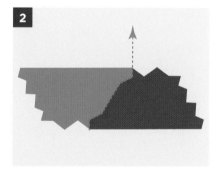

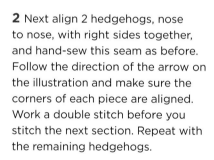

continued on page 72

Making the project bag

4 Using the template on the facing page as a guide, iron on the faces, following the manufacturer's instructions.

5 Place the patchwork panel, right side up, in the center of the right side of the outer fabric and pin. Machine-sew around the edge of the panel using a thread that coordinates with 1 fabric and a zigzag stitch.

6 Topstitch around the faces, using a straight stitch and the same thread as for the bodies, leaving a ¼-in. (0.5cm) seam allowance.

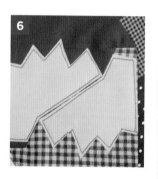

7 Press down a ¾-in. (2cm) seam allowance on the short edges of the outer fabric and 1 long edge of the lining fabrics. Place the outer fabric on a work surface with the right side down, and position the zipper in the center of 1 short edge. Place the batting on top, then add 1 piece of lining fabric, aligning the folded edge with the zipper; pin. Using a sewing machine fitted with a zipper foot and working on the right side of the fabric, topstitch the zipper, stitching all the layers. Repeat on the other side of the zipper.

8 Create the darts to make the sloping sides at the top of the project bag. Fold the project bag in half widthwise, so that the lining is on one side and the outer fabric and batting on the other. Using tailor's chalk or an erasable fabric pen, mark a point on the side of the project bag 1¼ in. (3cm) from the seam where the outer and lining fabrics meet. Machine-sew from this point to the end of the zipper. Repeat on the other side.

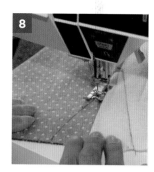

9 Machine-sew the sides of the project bag from the top (where the zipper is) to 3 in. (7.5cm) from the bottom, leaving a ⅜-in. (1cm) seam allowance.

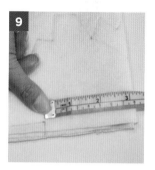

10 To shape the flat base of the project bag, open up the bottom and then fold in the opposite direction. Machine-sew each side in place, leaving a ⅜-in. (1cm) seam allowance. Repeat steps 8–10 for the lining.

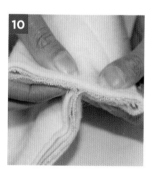

11 Turn the project bag right side out through the unstitched long edges of the lining. Use tailor's chalk or an erasable fabric pen to mark the position of the eyes. Use a seam ripper or the tip of a pair of scissors to make a hole for each eye. Push the shaft of the eye through the hole in the batting from the front to the back. Push on the washer until it is secure.

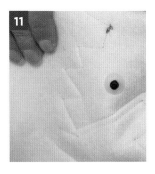

Finishing Off

12 Tuck in the raw edges of the lining fabric and hand-sew the gap closed, using a ladder stitch (see page 121) and a coordinating colored thread.

Hedgehog Templates

Template shown at 80%; enlarge to 100% before cutting out.

For information about cutting out the template and fabric shapes, see pages 109–111.

Fabric cutting line

– – – – – – –

Template cutting line

––––––––

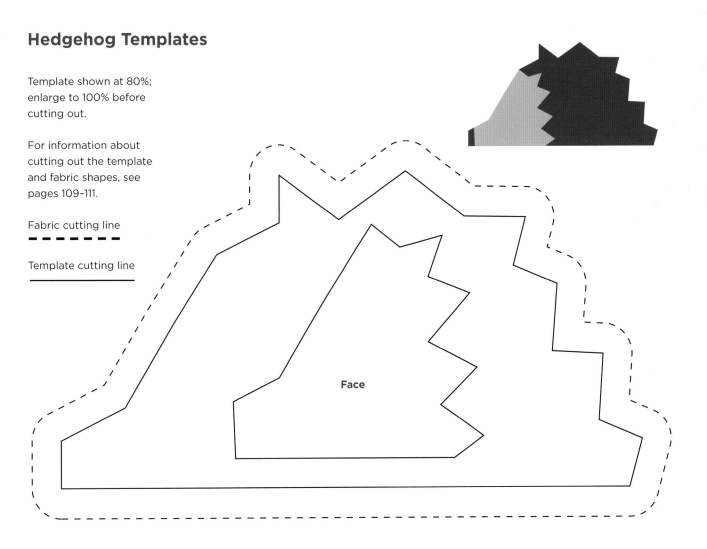

Face

Fox Seat Pad

These clever foxes fit perfectly onto this seat pad cover to bring a splash of color—and comfort—to any chair. Ribbon ties help to hold the seat pad in place.

You will need

8 Fox Templates (see page 77) cut from thin cardboard or heavy paper stock

4 pieces of fabric (white, orange, beige and brown) each measuring 11 x 12 in. (28 x 30cm) for the patchwork

2 pieces of fabric measuring 17 in. (43cm) square for the seat pad

60 in. (150cm) of 1-in. (2.5cm) wide ribbon for the seat ties

12-in. (30cm) zipper

16-in. (40.5cm) square pillow form

tailor's chalk or erasable fabric pen

ruler

contrasting colored thread for basting

coordinating colored thread for sewing

ball-headed pins

hand-sewing needle

sewing machine

Cutting out

8 fox shapes, 2 from each fabric. Baste them to the cardboard shapes (see page 113).

Two 30-in. (75cm) lengths of ribbon

Difficulty rating

Intermediate

Finished size

16 in. (40.5cm) square

Sewing the fox shapes

1 Decide on the arrangement of the fox shapes (see page 114). Hand-sew the foxes together in pairs, right sides together, from nose to tail along the tops of the bodies. Sew the tip of one fox's tail to the nose of the other fox, following the direction of the arrow on the illustration. Use a coordinating colored thread and a whipstitch, and finish with a double stitch (see page 114).

2 Next align the tail of one pair of foxes with the underside of another pair, right sides together, and hand-sew this seam as before. Follow the direction of the arrow on the illustration and make sure the corners of each piece are aligned. Work a double stitch before you stitch the next section. Repeat with the remaining pairs.

3 When you have sewn the 2 pairs of foxes together, hand-sew the sets of 4 together to create a square shape. Refer to your design arrangement for color placement. Whipstitch along the tails and undersides of the shapes with right sides together. You should have a panel approximately 15 in. (38cm) square.

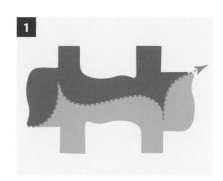

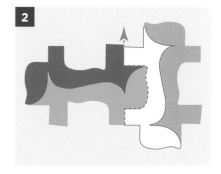

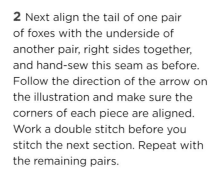

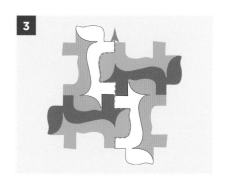

continued on page 76

Making the seat pad

4 Remove the basting stitches and pieces of cardboard from the patchwork panel. Press the seams flat on the wrong side.

5 Place the patchwork panel, right side up, in the center of the right side of 1 piece of seat pad fabric. Pin, then stitch the panel to the fabric by machine, using a zigzag stitch and a thread that coordinates with one of the patchwork fabrics.

6 Place the pieces of fabric for the seat pad, right sides together. Press down a ¾-in. (2cm) seam allowance on 1 edge of each piece. Place the fabrics side by side, with right sides down, on a work surface and position the zipper in the center of the prepared seams. Pin in place. Using a sewing machine fitted with a zipper foot and working on the right side of the fabric, topstitch the zipper in place, stitching along each side of the zipper and working three or four stitches across the bottom end to secure it (see page 119).

7 Pin, baste and then machine-stitch a ¼-in. (0.5cm) double-turned hem (see page 120) on each end of the lengths of ribbon. Fold the ribbons in half widthwise and position the folded ends so that they are centered between the ends of the zipper and the corners of the seat pad. Machine-stitch from the ends of the zipper to the corners of the fabric, to secure the ribbons, and sew the seam, leaving a ¾-in. (2cm) seam allowance.

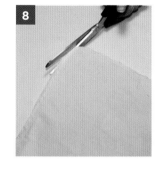

8 Open the zipper. Pin the remaining three sides of the cover, right sides together, then machine-sew around them, leaving a ¾-in. (2cm) seam allowance. Be sure the ends of the ribbon are not caught in the stitching. Trim the seam allowance to ⅜ in. (1cm), and trim the corners so that they will create sharp points when the cover is turned right side out. Iron the seams.

Finishing off

9 Turn the cover right side out through the zipper and press the seams. Insert the pillow form.

Tip

You can also hand-stitch the patchwork panel to the seat pad using a whipstitch (see page 114). Add extra color to the design by using a different contrasting colored thread for each patchwork shape.

Fox Template

Template shown at 100%

For information about cutting out the template and fabric shapes, see pages 109–111.

Fabric cutting line
— — — — —

Template cutting line
——————

Use the ribbon ties you have created to attach the cushion to the back of a dining chair.

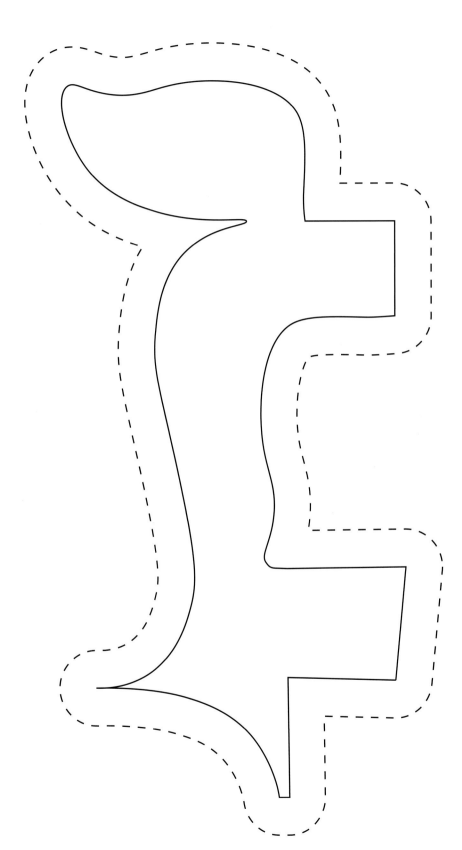

Teddy Bear Blanket

These happy teddy bears will keep youngsters warm and comfy. The appliquéd and embroidered faces give the bears a friendly appearance, while their hands stand proud of the fabric for added fun.

You will need

16 Teddy Bear Templates (see page 81) cut from thin cardboard or heavy paper stock

1 piece of pale brown fleece fabric measuring 20 x 60 in. (50 x 150cm) for the patchwork

1 piece of dark brown fleece fabric measuring 12 x 16 in. (30 x 40.5cm) for the ears

1 piece of fleece fabric measuring 24 x 28 in. (61 x 71cm) for the backing

1 piece of batting measuring 23 x 27 in. (58.5 x 68.5cm)

16 pairs of ½-in. (1.25cm) black plastic safety eyes

seam ripper

tailor's chalk or erasable fabric pen

ruler

contrasting colored thread for basting

coordinating colored thread for sewing

brown embroidery floss for the noses and mouths

ball-headed pins

hand-sewing needle

sewing machine

Cutting out

16 bear shapes from the pale brown fleece. Baste them to the cardboard shapes (see page 113).

32 ear shapes from the dark brown fleece.

Difficulty rating

Intermediate

Finished size

22 x 25½ in. (56 x 65cm)

Sewing the bear shapes

1 Hand-sew the bears together in pairs, right sides together, starting at the feet and working up toward the heads, following the direction of the arrow on the illustration (for clarity the bears shown in the illustration are different colors). Use a coordinating colored thread and a whipstitch, and finish with a double stitch (see page 114). Sew the hands together so that they stand proud of the bodies.

2 Sew pairs of bears together as before to make a row of four bears. Continue to hand-sew pairs together, following the direction of the arrow on the illustration, and making sure the corners of each piece are aligned. Work a double stitch before you stitch the next section. Sew 2 rows together along the top and bottom of each row as before, with right sides facing, to make a patchwork panel that is 2 bears tall by 4 bears wide.

3 Sew the 2 panels together, following the direction of the arrow on the illustration to create a panel that measures approximately 23 x 27 in. (58.5 x 68.5cm).

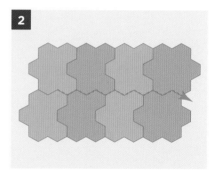

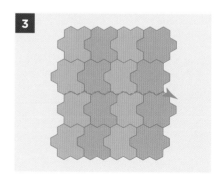

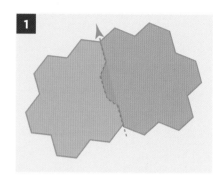

continued on page 80

Making the blanket

4 Clip the seam allowances. Remove the basting stitches and pieces of cardboard from the patchwork panel. Press the seams open on the wrong side. Use tailor's chalk or an erasable fabric pen to mark the details on the bears' faces (see the Teddy Bear Template). Pin, then baste the ears into position, then backstitch in place using a coordinating sewing thread (see page 123). Secure the thread ends on the wrong side of the fabric.

5 Use a seam ripper or the tip of a pair of scissors to make a hole for each eye. Push the shaft of the safety eye through the hole in the fleece from the front to the back. Push on the washer until it is secure.

6 Embroider the mouths, using brown embroidery floss, and backstitch as before. Then use the same floss and satin stitch (see page 124) to embroider the noses. Secure the thread on the wrong side of the fabric.

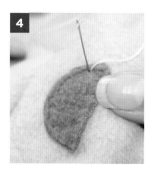

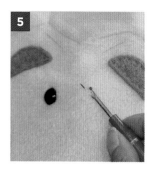

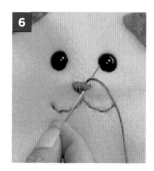

7 Place the backing fabric on a work surface with the wrong side facing up. Place the patchwork panel on top with the right side facing up. Use tailor's chalk or an erasable fabric pen to mark around the edge of the panel, including a ½-in. (1.25cm) seam allowance. Cut out the backing fabric along the marked lines.

8 Place the teddy bear panel on a work surface, right side up. Place the batting on top, followed by the backing fabric, with the right side facing down. Align the edges. Pin the layers together. Machine-sew around the edges, leaving a ⅜-in. (1cm) seam allowance and a 6-in. (15cm) gap in the bottom edge.

Finishing off

9 Trim the seam allowance to ¼ in. (0.5cm), and cut the corners at an angle so that they will not be bulky. Turn the blanket right side out through the gap. Tuck in the raw edges and ladder stitch the gap closed using a coordinating colored thread (for clarity, a contrasting colored thread has been used for the photograph).

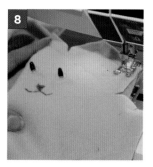

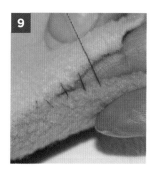

Teddy Bear Templates

Use this drawing as a template for the ears and as a guide to the position of the ears, nose and mouth.

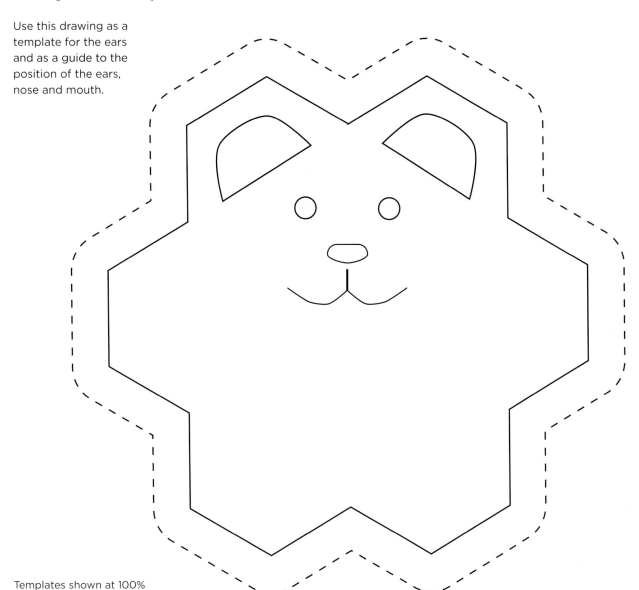

Templates shown at 100%

For information about cutting out the template and fabric shapes, see pages 109–111.

Fabric cutting line

Template cutting line

Wild Animals

Life in the wild can be amazing—swinging through the trees with the monkeys, visiting a water hole with the elephants, swooping through the skies with the birds and basking in the sun with the lizards. The bulletin board, tablet case, place mat and pillow shown here all celebrate these wonders of nature.

Elephant Bulletin Board

Elephants never forget—or so the saying goes—and neither will you with a fun elephant bulletin board to help keep track of all those important reminders. The pins used for the elephants' eyes will also hold your notes.

You will need

16 Elephant Templates (see page 87) cut from thin cardboard or heavy paper stock

4 pieces of fabric measuring 21 in. (53.5cm) square for the patchwork

1 piece of batting measuring 20 x 16 in. (50 x 40.5cm) for the backing

16 x 12-in. (40.5 x 30cm) cork bulletin board

16 berry pins

tailor's chalk or erasable fabric pen

ruler

contrasting colored thread for basting

coordinating colored thread for sewing

hand-sewing needle

duct tape

staple gun

Cutting out

16 elephants, 4 from each fabric. Baste them to the cardboard shapes (see page 113).

Difficulty rating

Easy

Finished size

16 x 12 in. (40.5 x 30cm)

Sewing the elephant shapes

1 Decide on the arrangement of the elephant shapes (see page 114). Hand-sew the elephants together in pairs, right sides together, starting with the heads. Sew the top of one head to the bottom of another, working toward the tail and following the direction of the arrow on the illustration. Use a coordinating colored thread and a whipstitch, and finish with a double stitch (see page 114).

2 Next join the pairs of elephants together as before to make 4 columns of 4 elephants, hand-sewing the seams as before. Follow the direction of the arrow on the illustration and make sure the corners of each piece are aligned. Work a double stitch before you stitch the next section.

3 Hand-sew the columns together. Refer to your design arrangement for color placement. Whipstitch along the heads and tails, with right sides together. Remove the basting stitches and pieces of cardboard. Press the seams open on the wrong side. The patchwork panel should measure approximately 20 x 16 in. (50 x 40.5cm).

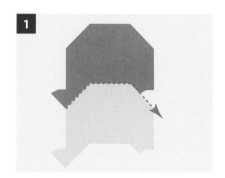

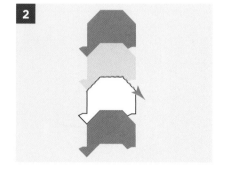

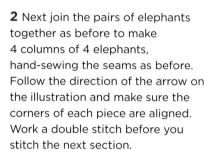

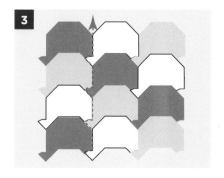

continued on page 86

Making the bulletin board

4 Following the template on the facing page, mark the ears using tailor's chalk or an erasable fabric pen. Place the batting on a work surface with the patchwork panel on top, right side up. Pin the edges. Use a sewing machine and a contrasting colored thread to embroider the ears, using a tight zigzag stitch.

5 Cover the bulletin board with the panel, making sure the fabric and batting are straight. To do this, place the panel on a work surface, right side down, and position the board on top so that it is centered. Use strips of duct tape to secure the center of the top and bottom edges. Check the position of the elephants, and adjust if necessary. Use a staple gun to attach the panel in the center of the top and bottom edges and check the position again. Work along the top and bottom edges, rolling the batting and fabric over the edge of the board rather than pulling it so that it keeps its shape. Repeat for the sides, folding the corners over carefully for a neat finish.

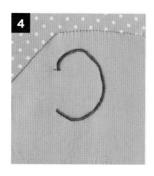

6 Trim the excess fabric from the back to leave a ⅜-in. (1cm) seam allowance.

Finishing off

7 Turn the bulletin board over and add berry pins for the elephants' eyes.

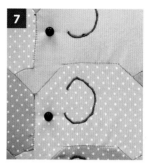

Tip

Before you start to staple the patchwork panel to the cork bulletin board, use additional strips of duct tape to hold it in place while you check the position. Remove the tape when you have finished stapling the fabric to the board.

Elephant Template

Template shown at 100%

For information about cutting out the template and fabric shapes, see pages 109–111.

Fabric cutting line

- - - - - - -

Template cutting line

————————

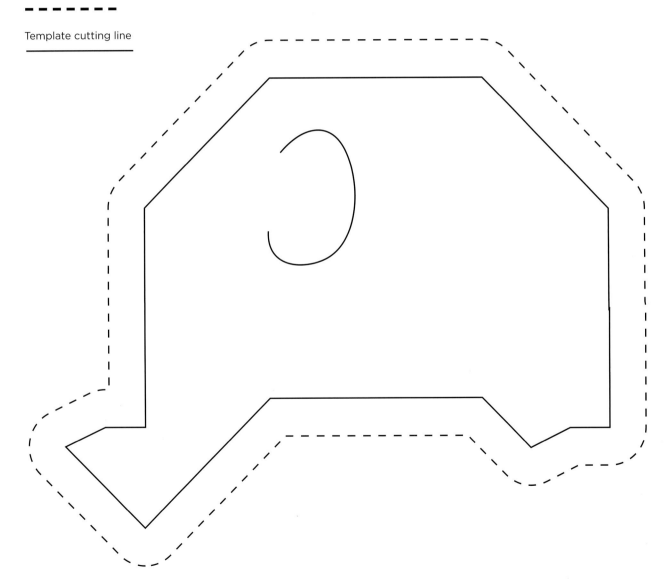

Monkey Tablet Sleeve

There's more to these mischievous monkeys than meets the eye. They decorate a practical tablet sleeve that will protect your device but also hide a clever secret—a pocket on the front to hold a pen and a pencil.

You will need

17 Monkey Templates (see page 91) cut from thin cardboard or heavy paper stock

4 pieces of fabric measuring 8 x 20 in. (20 x 50cm) for the patchwork

1 piece of fabric measuring 7½ x 11½ in. (19 x 29cm for the central panel

1 piece of fabric measuring 22 x 7½ in. (56 x 19cm) for the lining

1 piece of fabric measuring 7½ x 4 in. (19 x 10cm) for the pocket

1 piece of fabric measuring 5 x 5 in. (13 x 13cm) for the faces and ears

1 piece of batting measuring 22 x 7½ in. (56 x 19cm)

fusible web

tailor's chalk or erasable fabric pen

ruler

black embroidery floss for the eyes

contrasting colored thread for basting

coordinating colored thread for sewing

ball-headed pins

hand-sewing needle

sewing machine

Cutting out

17 monkey shapes, 4 from the patchwork fabrics and 1 from the pocket fabric. Baste them to the cardboard shapes (see page 113).

Back the fabric for the faces and ears with fusible web, following the manufacturer's instructions, and cut out 17 faces and 17 pairs of ears.

Difficulty rating

Intermediate

Finished size

8 x 11 in. (20 x 28cm)

Sewing the monkey shapes

1 Set aside the monkey for the pocket. Decide on the arrangement of the remaining 16 monkey shapes (see page 114). Hand-sew these monkeys together in pairs, right sides together. Start by sewing one monkey's shoulder to the top of the second monkey's arm, then continue around the top of the body, following the direction of the arrow on the illustration. Use a coordinating colored thread and a whipstitch, and finish each section of the shape with a double stitch (see page 114).

2 Sew the pairs of monkeys together as before to make 4 columns of 4 monkeys. Refer to your design arrangement for color placement. Whipstitch along the base of each shape with right sides together.

3 Sew 2 columns of monkeys together as before. Repeat with the remaining columns to make 2 columns that are 2 monkeys wide by 4 monkeys tall and measure approximately 19 x 7½ in. (48.5 x 19cm). Iron the back so that the panels lie flat.

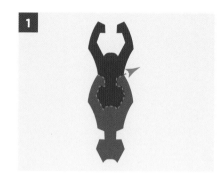

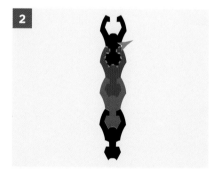

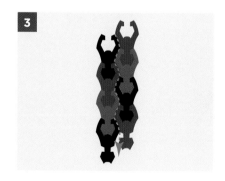

continued on page 90

Making the tablet cover

4 Following the manufacturer's instructions, attach the faces and ears to the monkeys using fusible web. Make the eyes using embroidery floss and French knots (see page 124) and position them as shown on the Monkey Templates. Remove the basting and cardboard from the left-hand side of one panel of monkeys and the right-hand side of the other. Press the seams flat on the wrong side.

5 Position the monkeys without cardboard on each side of the central panel fabric, with the seam allowance tucked under and the elbows aligned; pin in place so the panel measures 16 in. (40.5cm) wide. Use a sewing machine and contrasting colored thread to topstitch each panel ¼ in. (0.5cm) from the edge to join them.

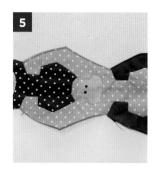

6 Remove the basting stitches and cardboard from the pocket. Baste the seam allowance to the wrong side. Using a coordinating colored thread and a sewing machine, topstitch across the top of the head ¼ in. (0.5cm) from the edge (see page 117).

7 Position the pocket monkey in the center of the central panel; pin, then baste in place. Use a sewing machine and coordinating colored thread to topstitch around the monkey ¼ in. (0.5cm) from the edge as before, leaving the head section open.

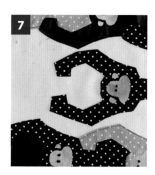

8 Fold the patchwork panel in half widthwise, with right sides facing, and hand-sew the monkey panels together, using whipstitch as before. Remove the remaining basting stitches and cardboard. Press on the wrong side with the seams open, so that the central panel is in the center of one side of the patchwork.

9 Pin the bottom edges of the panel together to make the outside of the cover. Use a sewing machine and a coordinating colored thread to sew a ½-in. (1.25cm) seam. Turn right side out.

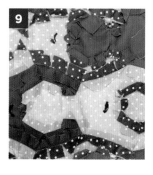

10 Position the batting against the wrong side of the lining fabric and pin around the edges. Use a sewing machine and a coordinating colored thread to sew around the edge, leaving a ½-in. (1.25 cm) seam allowance and a 3-in. (7.5cm) gap in one side.

11 Insert the patchwork cover (right side out) inside the lining (wrong side out). Align, then pin the raw edges. Use a sewing machine and a coordinating colored thread to sew the edges, leaving a ½-in. (1.25cm) seam allowance.

Finishing off

13 Use a sewing machine and contrasting colored thread to topstitch around the opening of the cover ¼ in. (0.5cm) from the edge as before.

12 Turn the cover right side out through the gap in the lining. Tuck in the raw edges and use a ladder stitch and a co-ordinating thread to sew the gap closed. Press the fabric. Push the lining into the tablet sleeve.

Monkey Templates

Templates shown at 80%; enlarge to 100% before cutting out.

For information about cutting out the template and fabric shapes, see pages 109–111.

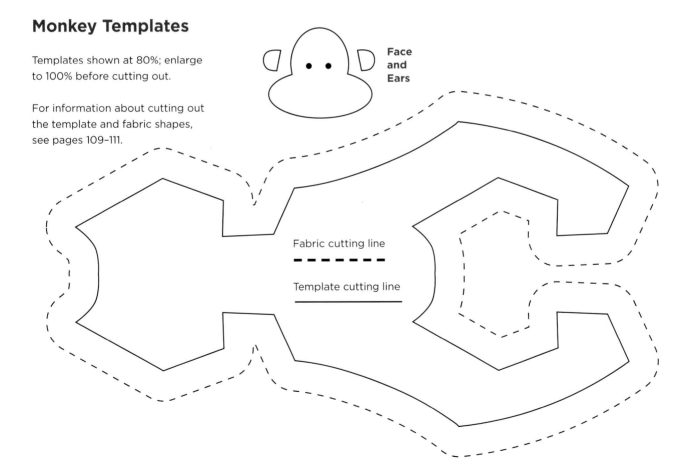

Face and Ears

Fabric cutting line

Template cutting line

Lizard Pillow

This comfy pillow is covered with scampering lizards. It will add a burst of color to a hall bench or kitchen chair to transform it into the perfect spot for lounging on a lazy afternoon. Or take it outside to use on a garden chair or bench.

You will need

24 Lizard Templates (see page 95) cut from thin cardboard or heavy paper stock

4 pieces of fabric measuring 16 x 16 in. (40.5 x 40.5cm) for the patchwork

2 pieces of fabric measuring 10 x 10 in. (25 x 25cm) for the border

1 piece of fabric measuring 40 x 20 in. (100 x 50cm) for the backing

16-in. (40.5cm) round pillow form insert, 2 in. (5cm) thick

tailor's chalk or erasable fabric pen

ruler

tape measure

contrasting colored thread for basting

coordinating colored thread for sewing

ball-headed pins

hand-sewing needle

sewing machine

Cutting out

24 lizard shapes, 6 from each of the patchwork fabrics. Baste them to the cardboard shapes (see page 113).

Eighteen 3-in. (7.5cm) squares for the border, 9 from each of the border fabrics.

17½-in. (44.5cm) diameter semicircle and 17½-in. (44.5cm) circle for the pillow backing. Trim 4 in. (10cm) from one side of the circle.

Difficulty rating

Intermediate

Finished size

16 in. (40.5cm) diameter

Sewing the lizard shapes

1 Decide on the arrangement of the lizard shapes (see page 114). Hand-sew a pair of lizards together, right sides together, starting with the legs. Sew the tip of one lizard's right front leg to the gap between the other lizard's right front and back legs, following the direction of the arrow on the illustration. Use a coordinating colored thread and a whipstitch, and finish each section with a double stitch (see page 114). Continue to stitch along the sides of the bodies to join the side of the head to the side of the tail.

2 Join a third lizard to the pair. Start by joining one side of the head of the new lizard to the tail of one of the joined lizards, sewing as before. Continue to stitch along the sides of the bodies to join the new lizard to the second joined lizard. Repeat to join all of the lizards together in sets of 3.

3 When you have sewn the 18 lizards together in sets of 3, hand-sew the sets together to create a circle about 17 in. (43cm) in diameter. Refer to your design arrangement for color placement. Whipstitch along the sides of the bodies to join them together as before. Iron the back so that the panel lies flat.

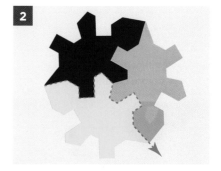

continued on page 94

Making the cover

4 Draw a circle 17½-in. (44.5cm) in diameter onto paper to use as a template (see Tip). Place the patchwork panel right side up on a work surface with the template in the center. Use tailor's chalk or an erasable fabric pen to draw around the template. Cut out along the marked lines. Remove the basting stitches and cardboard. Press the seams open on the wrong side.

5 Pin the squares for the border together in a row, alternating the colors. Use a sewing machine to join the squares, leaving a ¾-in. (2cm) seam allowance. Join the first and last squares to make a ring, being careful not to twist the strip.

6 Use a tape measure and pins to divide the circumference of the patchwork panel into quarters. Repeat on one long edge of the border. Align the pins for each quarter and pin the fabrics together at these points, with right sides facing. Pin the fabrics together between the pin markers. Use a sewing machine to join the panels, leaving a ¾-in. (2cm) seam allowance.

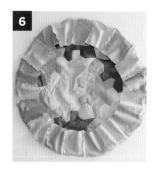

7 Use a sewing machine to stitch a double-turned hem (see page 120) along the straight edges of both sections of the backing, using a 1¼-in. (3cm) seam allowance.

8 Place the smaller back piece on a work surface, with the right side facing down. Then place the larger back piece on top, right side down, and align the edges to create a circle. Pin, then baste the layers together to hold them in place.

9 Use a tape measure and pins to divide the circumference of the pillow backing into quarters. Repeat on the edge of the border/patchwork panel to divide it into quarters. Align the pins for each quarter and pin the fabrics together at these points, with right sides facing. Pin the fabrics together between the pin markers, aligning the fabrics evenly. Baste, then use a sewing machine to join the seam, leaving a ¾-in. (2cm) seam allowance.

Finishing off

10 Remove the basting stitches holding the back panel sections together and turn the right side out through the gap. Insert the pillow form.

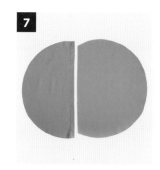

Lizard Template

Template shown at 100%

For information about cutting out the template and fabric shapes, see pages 109–111.

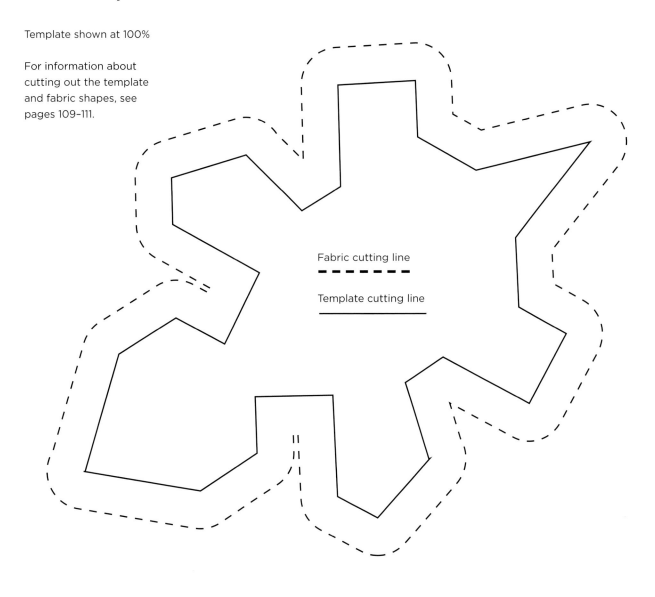

Fabric cutting line

- - - - - - -

Template cutting line

_____

Tip

Use a circular object 17½ in. (44.5cm) in diameter to make a template for the seat cushion. Suitable items might include the lid of a garbage can, a storage tub, or the pillow form itself. Place the item on a large sheet of paper—such as kraft paper or poster board—and draw around it. Cut out the template and use it as a guide to cutting out the fabric.

Bird Place Mat

This pretty bird place mat will brighten up any dinner table. Add a simple coaster to make a coordinated table setting.

You will need

12 Bird Templates (see page 99) cut from thin cardboard or heavy paper stock

4 pieces of fabric measuring 20 x 8 in. (50 x 20cm) for the patchwork

1 piece of fleece fabric measuring 20 x 18 in. (50 x 45cm) for the backing

1 piece of batting measuring 20 x 18 in. (50 x 45cm)

tailor's chalk or erasable fabric pen

ruler

contrasting colored thread for basting

coordinating colored thread for sewing

ball-headed pins

hand-sewing needle

sewing machine

Cutting out

12 bird shapes, 3 from each fabric; six of the birds must face to the left, and six to the right. Baste them to the cardboard shapes (see page 113).

Difficulty rating

Intermediate

Finished size

17½ x 16½ in. (44.5 x 41.5cm)

Sewing the bird shapes

1 Decide on the arrangement of the bird shapes (see page 114). Hand-sew the birds together in pairs, right sides together. Sew the head of one bird to the tail of another, working toward the head and wing tip and following the direction of the arrow on the illustration. Use a coordinating colored thread and a whipstitch, and finish with a double stitch (see page 114).

2 Next join the pairs of birds together, working from the wing tip to the head, to make 3 rows of 4 birds, hand-sewing the seam as before. Follow the direction of the arrow on the illustration and make sure the corners of each piece are aligned. Work a double stitch before you stitch the next section.

3 Hand-sew the rows together to create 3 columns of 4 birds. Refer to your design arrangement for color placement. Whipstitch along the edges with right sides together. Remove the basting stitches and pieces of cardboard. Press the seams open on the wrong side. The patchwork panel should measure approximately 18 x 17 in. (45 x 43cm).

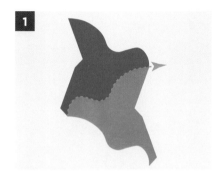

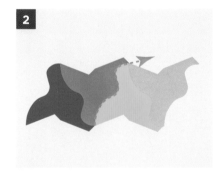

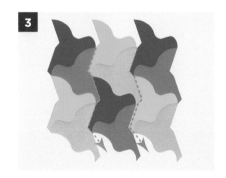

continued on page 98

Making the place mat

4 Place the batting on a work surface and place the backing fabric on top, with the right side facing down and edges aligned. Place the bird panel on top, right side facing down. Pin, then baste the layers together. Snip into the seam allowance curves, so that they will sit neatly when you sew and when the place mat is turned right side out.

5 Use a sewing machine to stitch around all four sides of the place mat, leaving a ¾-in. (2cm) seam allowance and a 6-in. (15cm) gap in one side to turn the mat the right side out. Sew the seam with the bird panel facing up, to allow you to keep the patchwork seams open. Trim the excess fabric to leave a ⅜-in. (1cm) seam allowance. Iron the seams open on the wrong side.

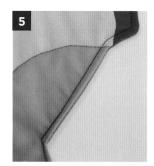

Finishing off

6 Turn the place mat right side out through the gap. Tuck in the raw edges and use a ladder stitch to sew the gap closed. Press the fabric. Use a sewing machine and coordinating colored thread to topstitch around the place mat ¼ in. (0.5cm) from the edge (see page 117).

Bird coaster

To make a matching coaster, cut 2 bird shapes from 2 pieces of fabric measuring 7 x 7 in. (18 x 18cm) and a bird shape from a piece of batting the same size. Place the batting on a work surface and place one bird shape on top, with the right side facing down. Place the second bird shape on top, right side facing down. Pin, then baste the layers together. Clip the curves so that they will create sharp points when the coaster is turned right side out. Use a sewing machine to stitch around the edges of the bird shapes, leaving a ¾-in. (2cm) seam allowance and a 2-in. (5cm) gap in one side. Trim the seam allowance to ⅜ in. (1cm). Turn the coaster right side out through the gap. Tuck in the raw edges and use a ladder stitch to sew the gap closed. Press the fabric. Use a sewing machine and coordinating colored thread to topstitch around the coaster ¼ in. (0.5cm) from the edge (see page 117).

Bird Template

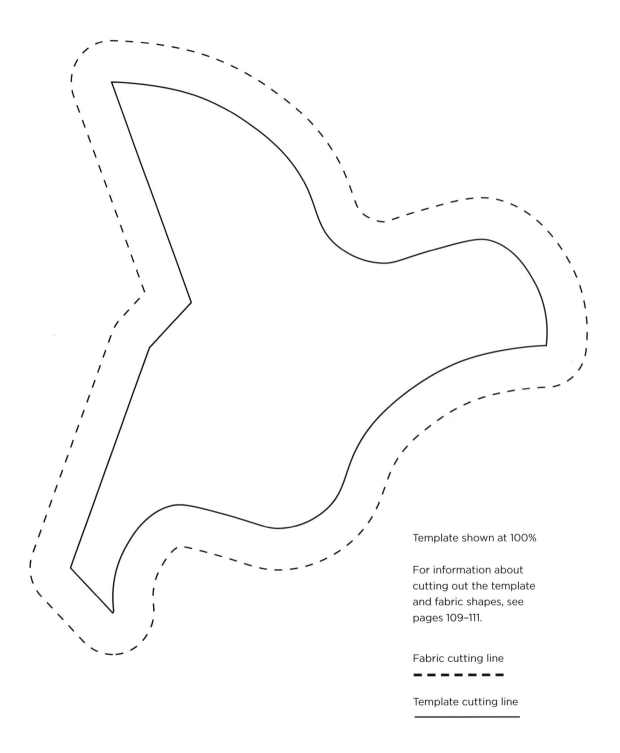

Template shown at 100%

For information about cutting out the template and fabric shapes, see pages 109–111.

Fabric cutting line
- - - - - - -

Template cutting line
————

Techniques

Discover how to cut out the templates and fabrics, the best stitches for sewing them together and how to decorate your patchwork with embroidery and appliqué. There are also tips on the best equipment to use.

Tools & Equipment

Patchwork requires some basic equipment—as long as you have scissors, pins, needles, thread, paper and fabrics you can tackle most of the projects in this book. A sewing machine will be useful but is not essential.

Threads

To sew patchwork shapes together you need two types of thread: basting and sewing.

Basting thread is used to attach the fabric shapes temporarily to the card sewing templates (see page 113). You can buy specialty basting thread which is inexpensive and breaks easily, making it quick and easy to cut through but unsuitable for permanent stitching. Alternatively, you can use any spare sewing thread you have. Ideally, the color of the basting thread will contrast with the fabrics you are using so it is easy to identify and remove after all the shapes have been stitched together.

Most work baskets contain a collection of sewing threads. Use spare thread to baste your patchwork.

To sew the shapes together you need a good quality sewing thread. Most of the projects in this book require you to hand-sew the seams. To do this you need a strong thread that can withstand a good level of tension, as you will pull the stitches tight to ensure the seams are invisible. It's very frustrating if you are using a thread that can't take the pressure and keeps snapping as you work. I find that polyester or cotton threads work well. You may be told that you should use a cotton thread with cotton fabrics, but I recommend you use a thread that is strong enough to take the tension of the stitches and is the best color match for the fabrics.

Do not be tempted to use too long a length of thread in your needle as it may knot or snap. A piece the length of your forearm should be about right and will not need replenishing too often.

Hand-sewing needles

There are a variety of different types of hand-sewing needles available, but for these patchwork projects, you will need the general-purpose needles known as "sharps." These have short, round threading eyes that provide added strength during sewing and that are easy to pull through the fabric as you sew.

Don't be tempted to use an old needle that has been in your work basket for a long time as it may not be sharp. Set aside needles to use for the basting only—needles will blunt as you push them through the cardboard templates and so become unsuitable for use with fabric.

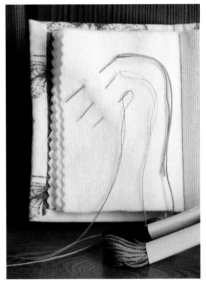

You will need needles for basting, hand-sewing and embroidery.

continued on page 104

Sewing machine

There are many sewing machines on the market, and if you are going to buy one, make sure that it features adjustable straight and zigzag stitches—it's important to be able to adjust stitch size to match the fabric you are using. If you want to try some machine embroidery, then look for a machine that will allow you to drop the feed dogs. These are the serrated teeth that sit under the sewing-machine foot and push the fabric along as you sew. If they can be dropped you can move the fabric around freestyle. You will also need a free-motion embroidery foot. A zipper foot is useful if you want to insert zippers in any projects or if you want to add piping and some other trims. A sewing machine with a buttonhole feature can also be very useful.

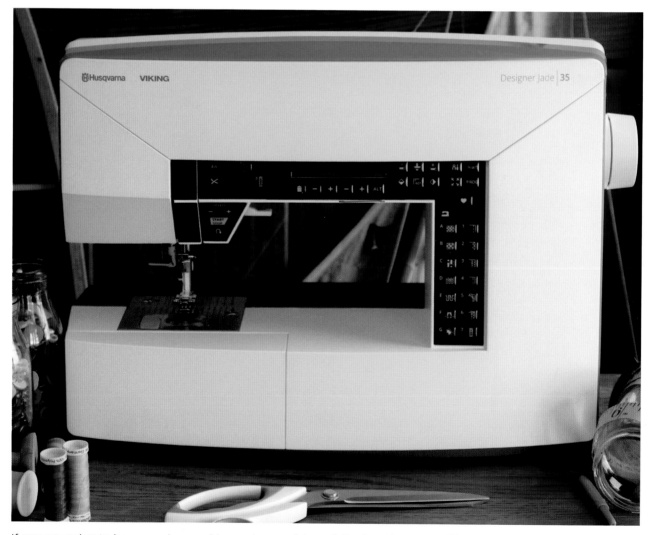

If you are going to buy a sewing machine make sure it has all the functions you will need.

Pins

Standard metal dressmaking pins are ideal for patchwork, but you may find that ball-headed ones are easier to insert and remove. If you are planning to use batting to quilt your patchwork (see page 117), then you may find that long quilter's pins, that will not become hidden in the layers, work best for you.

Scissors

The first rule of sewing is to use your fabric scissors only for cutting fabric; otherwise, they will quickly become blunt. As well as a pair of razor-sharp fabric scissors, you will need some general-purpose scissors for cutting out the cardboard templates—a pair with a sharp tip will enable you to cut into the corners—and a small pair of scissors for cutting threads.

Rotary cutter

If you need to cut out multiple straight-edged shapes, such as squares and triangles, you may find it easier to use a rotary cutter rather than scissors. Use it with a cutting mat and ruler to cut accurate straight lines.

Tape measure and ruler

These are essential for measuring fabrics and marking straight lines on the fabric.

Seam ripper

The curved blade of this small tool is traditionally used to remove stitches. However, the pointed tip also can be used to make holes in fabric to insert safety eyes.

Tailor's chalk and erasable fabric pens

Use these to mark fabric before you cut or embellish it. Tailor's chalk has a thin edge, enabling you to create detailed markings that can be brushed away. The ink from the erasable fabric pens can be dabbed off with water or will fade in the light. However, check that the ink will disappear from the fabrics you are using by testing the pens on a scrap before you begin.

You will need different scissors for different tasks. A rotary cutter will help to cut straight lines.

Mark cutting lines and seams using a ruler and tailor's chalk or an erasable fabric pen.

Fabrics

Choosing the fabrics you want to use for patchwork is one of the most exciting parts of the process. You may want colors, patterns and textures that complement each other, or those that provide a contrast.

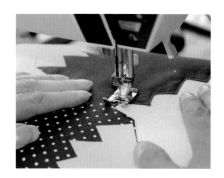

Fabrics that are a similar weight will be simpler to work with than a mixture of different weights.

People ask me all the time for advice about which fabrics to use and it comes down to personal preference; I tend to sew with a range of fabrics and am a great advocate of trying something new and even combining different types of fabric to create different effects and textures.

Patchwork is traditionally made from fabrics that are all the same weight, often a 100 percent cotton designed specifically for patchwork and quilting. This will give you a great finish, but it may not provide you with the range of colors and patterns you need or that will work with the patchwork design.

In this book I have used lots of different fabrics, from quilting cotton to fleece, cotton poplin to polycotton. I have even printed some fabrics to work with the templates and so do away with the need to embellish them. It doesn't matter which fabrics you choose, as long as you are comfortable working with them.

The piece of advice I always give is no matter what fabrics you are using, wash, dry and iron them before you begin. Then there is no risk that they will shrink or that the color will run when you wash the patchwork, spoiling your work.

If you want to mix different types of fabric, make sure they all can be washed in the same way; otherwise, you may find some sections survive the laundering process better than others. Because you need to sew the shapes together with small, hidden stitches, you may find it easier to work with tightly woven fabrics rather than ones with a looser weave, which could show the stitches. Tightly woven fabrics also are less likely to fray.

Plain fabrics will create blocks of color that really show off the designs. However, part of the fun of patchwork is putting together different patterns to create an exciting visual feast.

When choosing patterned fabrics, remember that smaller patterns work best for patchwork, as larger designs will often affect the way the eye views the shapes. Batiks and irregular patterns can work really well if you place the templates on the fabric carefully, the fabric can create interesting features, such as eyes, noses and ears, without having to sew or embroider them later.

If you have a stash of fabrics on hand, you will always have something to use for your patchwork projects.

Templates

Each patchwork piece is created using two cardboard templates: a larger cutting template, which is used to cut out the fabric pieces, and a smaller sewing template onto which the fabric is stitched.

To make your templates, you will need to transfer the relevant image for your project onto the cardboard you are using. Start by photocopying the template image or scan it and print it out. Cut around the outer dotted line of the template image on your printout. Use this to cut out one shape from your cardboard—this is the cutting template. Now cut around the solid line on your printout so you have a smaller shape. Use this to cut out shapes from your cardboard for the sewing templates—cut out as many as are needed for your project.

Most of the templates in the book are given at full size (100 percent) but if you need to enlarge them, do so on the photocopier (or scanner).

I always use a 160gsm cardboard for the templates as it will hold its shape when you sew through it. Do not be tempted to use thinner cardboard or paper as it doesn't have the strength to create the sharp corners you need when working with complex patchwork shapes. On the other hand, thick cardboard, such as that from a cereal box, is too stiff and will be difficult to get the needle through when basting the fabric to the shapes. Many of the shapes need to be folded as you sew them together and this is harder to do if you have used thicker cardboard. The number you will need is given at the start of each project.

The cutting template is ½ in. (1.25cm) larger all around than the sewing template to give you a seam allowance. The seam allowance is folded over the sewing template and the fabric is basted on (see page 112).

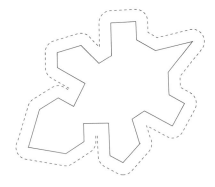

Each template has two outlines: The outer one for cutting out the fabric and the inner one for sewing the patchwork shapes.

Cut out the templates from cardboard—160gsm cardboard is stiff enough to hold its shape but flexible enough to stitch through.

Cutting Out the Fabric

Once you know how many shapes you need, arrange the cutting templates on the fabric before you start to cut them out, to make sure you can cut out all the shapes you require from each piece of fabric.

The projects in this book specify the number of shapes required, but if you want to create your own design you may need a different number. The shapes are irregular so there is no simple way to determine how many you will need. The best way to do this is to divide the width of the patchwork panel you plan to make by the width of the patchwork shape template, then add on the width of two more shapes to allow for any odd pieces you may need to fill in any gaps at the sides. Then do the same for the height of the panel. Multiply these two numbers together and you will have the number of shapes you need.

Place the cutting template on the grain of the fabric (see page 111).

Next you need to calculate how much fabric you will need and how to cut out the patchwork shapes from it. To do this you need to answer the following questions:

- How many shapes will I need?

- Do all of the shapes need to face the same direction?

- Will the pattern of the fabric work with my design?

Calculate the number of shapes

For example, using the dog template on page 23 to make a cover for an 18-in. (45cm) square pillow the calculation is as follows:

The dimensions of the dog template are
4¾ in. (12cm) wide by 4¾ in. (13cm) high.

Number of dogs wide =
(18 [45] divided by 4¾ [12]) +2 = 5.78, let's round it up to 6.

Number of dogs high =
(18 [45] divided by 4¾ [13]) +2 = 5.78, let's round it up to 6.

Number of dogs needed for the pillow =
6 dogs wide x 6 dogs high = 36

For most of the projects in this book, the animal shapes all face in the same direction; the instructions will tell you if you need to cut out shapes facing in two (opposite) directions (see the Bird Place Mat on page 96). Cut out the shapes on the grain of the fabric (see the facing page).

How much fabric?

The number of different fabrics you use for each design is up to you. I have used between one and four fabrics for the examples in the book, but you may want to use more colors and patterns than this. If you are using fabrics from your stash, you can place the template on each piece and work out how many dogs you can cut out, remembering to include a seam allowance. If you need to buy fabrics, then use the maximum width and height measurement for the shape to calculate the dimensions of the fabric you will need. For example, including a seam allowance, each dog needs a piece of fabric measuring 5⅛ in. (13cm) square. If you want to use two fabrics for the pillow cover, you will need to cut 18 from each one.

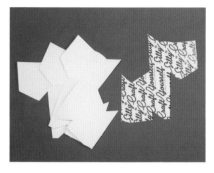

Work out how many shapes you will need before cutting out the templates or the fabric.

Patchwork and quilting fabrics are usually sold from rolls 44 in. (112cm) wide, but you can buy precut pieces known as fat quarters. These are designed for patchwork and measure 18 x 22 in. (45 x 56cm). They are often sold in packs of coordinating colors and patterns, making them ideal for beginners. If you want to use "fat quarters" for your pillow, you could cut out two dogs from each quarter, meaning you would need 18 fat quarters, nine of each fabric. If you are going to use fabric from a roll, you need to work out how many dogs (including a seam allowance) will fit the width of the fabric.

Each dog is 4 in. (10cm) wide.
44 in. (112cm) divided by 4¾ in. (12cm) = 9.3 so you can fit 9 whole dogs across the width of a length of fabric, and you will need to cut two rows of eight dogs.

Each dog measures 5 in. (13cm) high and so two rows will measure 10¼ in. (26cm) of fabric (5⅛ in. [13cm] x 2 = 10¼ in. (26cm). So, you will need 10¼ in. (26cm) of fabric.

Include seam allowance

Unless they are used for appliqué (see page 116), all the fabrics used in this book require a seam allowance. The size of the allowance is marked on the templates or listed in the instructions.

Cutting out the shapes

Cut out the shapes on the grain of the fabric. This means the shapes are positioned parallel to the lengthwise or widthwise threads used to weave the fabric. This will ensure the shapes are stable after they are sewn together. If the shapes are cut on the diagonal of the fabric (referred to as "on the bias"), they will stretch out of shape.

To cut out the fabric, place the cutting template onto the fabric and draw around it using tailor's chalk or an erasable fabric pen. Repeat until you have the desired number of shapes. Cut out the shapes along the marked lines. If you want to use certain parts of a patterned fabric, make a cutting template with the center removed so that you can see the section of the pattern that will feature that shape.

Once you know how many shapes you need, decide how you would like to arrange them; then all you need to do is sew them together.

Preparing the Fabric Shapes

Take time to baste the fabric to the sewing templates so that the shapes are easy to sew together. Make sure the seam allowances are folded neatly on the wrong side and secured in position.

Once you have cut out the fabric shapes, pin them onto the sewing templates so that the templates are in the center of the fabric. Fold the seam allowance over the edges of the templates and baste it in place. This is one of the most important stages in paper-piecing patchwork. It's straightforward when you are working with simple shapes such as hexagons, but there are a few extra things to think about when working with more complicated shapes. These techniques require a little practice, but once you have made a couple you should find them easy to do.

Take time to fold the fabric to the wrong side and baste it in place neatly as this will help to create a neat finish to your project.

Basting stitch

The stitch used to baste the fabric to the cardboard is an ordinary running stitch. You can use large stitches for this, as long as they hold the fabric in place, and they will be quicker to sew. You will need to remove the stitches and cardboard before sewing the project together. Do not loop the thread around the edge of the paper pieces as this will make it trickier when it is time to sew the pieces together.

You will need to cut into curved seams so that they lie flat.

Basting straight edges
You will only need a couple of stitches to hold the fabric in place.

External corners
Fold the seam allowance over itself to cover the template. When it comes to narrow angles, don't be tempted to cut off the excess as you may need it when you are sewing the shapes together. You can trim it off once the pieces have been sewn together.

Internal corners
When working corners that bend inward, you will need to clip into the seam allowance to allow the fabric to move into the corner. Do this carefully as you don't want to snip too far. If you're worried about the fabric fraying, stop $\frac{1}{16}$ in. (0.2cm) short of the corner. When basting internal corners, make sure your thread does not span the gap, which will make sewing the pieces together more difficult. If you do cut too far into the corners all is not lost; use some of the extra fabric you left on the outer corners to rescue any overzealous snipping.

External curves
Treat these in the same way as external corners, but rather than folding the seam allowance to make a sharp corner, pleat it as you stitch to make several small folds.

Internal curves
These work following the same principal as the external curves, but with small snips to allow for movement within the fabric.

Handpiecing

Once all of your patchwork pieces have been prepared, you're all set for the best bit—sewing them together and watching your design take shape.

Before you start

Before you start to sew, plan your design by arranging the shapes in position on a work surface. This allows you to find the best combination of colors and patterns. When you are happy with the arrangement of your shapes, take a photograph for reference when it comes time to sew the shapes together.

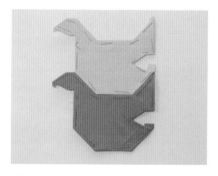

Check the arrangement of the shapes before you begin

Whipstitch

The shapes are sewn with right sides together, using a whipstitch and a coordinating colored thread that will not be visible on the finished item.

To work a whipstitch, secure the end of the thread by making two small stitches at the edge of one of the shapes. Insert the needle through both fabric shapes, just below the folded edge. Repeat, inserting the thread from the same side each time, so that the thread goes over the edges to hold the shapes together, making the stitches ¼ in. (0.5cm) apart. Repeat until you reach the end of the section.

To make your stitches less visible, only sew into the tiniest bit of fabric from each of the shapes—the smaller the piece of fabric you work with, the less your stitches will show at the front. Tension is really important: Too loose and your stitches will be more visible; too tight and you risk snapping threads and the seam will pucker.

Each whipstitch should "catch" two or three threads in the fabric.

Joining straight edges

Most of the shapes are designed with short straight edges to make the sewing a little easier. The best way to work is to align the corners on the edge you are about to sew, folding the shapes if it makes this easier, then whipstitch the edges together. When you get to a corner, add a double stitch for security. Unfold the cardboard shapes and then refold before sewing the next seam.

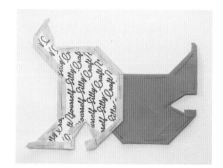

Change the position of the shapes as you sew each seam.

Joining curved seams

To sew a curved seam, you can either sew short sections at a time, folding and manipulating the shape as you go, or stitch the curve with the two shapes held flat and side by side. The method you use is up to you, but if you work the curved edges flat you will have to do less repositioning as you sew. Use a whipstitch as before, but rather than holding them with right sides facing, position the pieces so they are aligned as they will be on the finished item. Stitch into the edges of the shapes, rather than over them, and make sure your tension is even.

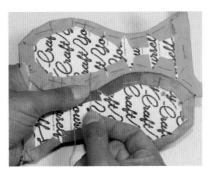

Hold curved shapes side by side and then sew them together.

Removing the cardboard shapes

Once you have finished sewing your shapes together, you will need to remove the cardboard. Simply use a seam ripper or small pair of scissors to snip the basting stitches; then gently pull out the cardboard.

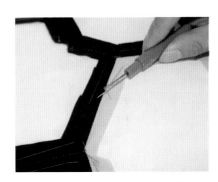

Use a seam ripper to remove the basting stitches.

Finishing Off

Once you have completed the patchwork, you can embellish it before completing the project. The ideas in this book use appliqué, quilting and stitching to achieve this. Finally, it's important to press your work.

Appliqué

This form of decoration involves attaching pieces of fabric to a backing fabric to create a design. You can do this using iron-on fusible web, or using hand- or machine-stitching.

To use fusible web, follow the manufacturer's instructions on the packaging. You will need to use an iron to "melt" the adhesive on the web and attach it to the fabric.

If you want to use a sewing machine, baste the shape in place first. Sew the shape using a zigzag stitch $\frac{1}{16}$ in. (0.2cm) tall and with the stitches close together—$\frac{1}{32}$ in. (0.1cm) is ideal. Stitch around the edge of the appliqué shape to secure it and hide the raw edges.

If you plan to hand-stitch the shapes into place, baste them and use a whipstitch (see page 114) around the edge of the shape.

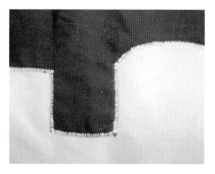

A short and tight machine zigzag stitch is ideal for stitching appliqué.

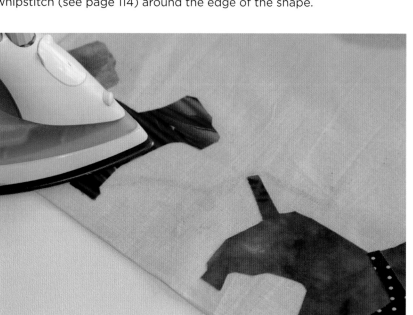

You will need an iron to attach appliqué shapes using fusible web.

Topstitching

You can decorate the edges of your patchwork, or join the patchwork to the backing fabric, using topstitching. As the name suggests, this stitch is worked on top of the fabric. You can sew by hand, using a running stitch or backstitch (see page 123), or use your sewing machine and a straight stitch. Make sure the stitches are an even distance from the edge of the patchwork—¼ in. (0.5cm) is ideal—all the way around. They should follow the outline of the shape and be of an equal length.

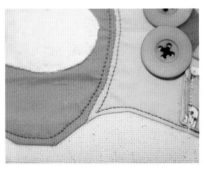

Use a contrasting color thread to show off your topstitching.

Quilting

Quilted fabric provides insulation and cushioning. It is created by sandwiching a layer of batting between two layers of fabric and stitching them together. The projects in this book that use batting are stitched around the edges. However, you can also topstitch patterns into the surface of the "sandwich" to further enhance the design.

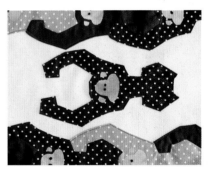

A combination of appliqué and topstitching provides visual interest.

Pressing

To ensure a neat finish, it is important to press the seams as you work. The instructions for each project will tell you when to do this to ensure that the seams sit correctly on the finished item.

Fastenings

If you are making a portfolio or pillow cover and want to ensure the contents do not fall out, you may choose to add a fastening such as Velcro®, a zipper or buttons. Buttons can also be used as a form of decoration (see the Owl Portfolio on page 66).

Buttons

To sew on a button, thread a needle with sewing thread or, if the button is decorative, with embroidery floss. Make a few small stitches on the wrong side of the fabric to secure the thread, and then take the needle through to the right side of the fabric in the position of the button. Insert the needle through one hole in the button from the back to front, and then insert it from front to back into the opposite hole and the back of the fabric. If the button has two holes for the thread, keep working through them until the button is secure. If the button has four holes, work the stitches diagonally to make an X shape, alternating the direction, until it is secure. Finish the button by sewing a few small stitches at the back of the fabric.

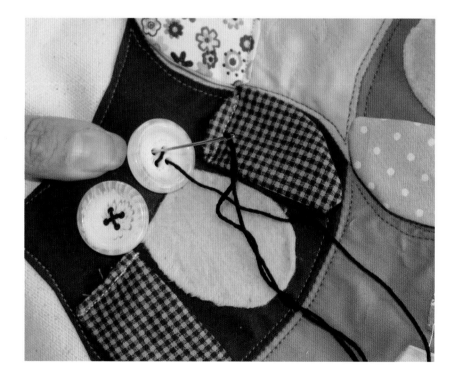

Use buttons to create a three-dimensional decorative finish.

Press stud or snap fasteners

These metal or plastic fasteners are sewn onto two sides of an opening to hold them together. Make a few small stitches on the wrong side of the fabric to secure the thread, and then take the needle through to the right side of the fabric, in the position of the fastener. Each half has four holes. Sewing through one hole at a time, use a whipstitch to secure the two pieces in place. Finish with a few small stitches at the back of the fabric.

Velcro

This fastening consists of two tapes—one with small fabric hooks, the other with small fabric loops—that grip each other when pressed together. Decide on the position of the tape and cut a piece to the desired length. Sew each tape into position using a whipstitch (see page 114) around the edges.

Zipper

To insert a zipper into the back of a seat pad cover, measure the length of the zipper and mark this distance in the center of the seam where the zipper will sit. Machine-sew the seams at each end of the zipper and baste across the opening where the zipper will go (this will make it easier to press open the seam). Press the seam open on the wrong side and remove the basting stitches. Position the zipper face down in the gap in the seam. Pin, then baste in place. Using a sewing machine fitted with a zipper foot and working on the right side of the fabric, topstitch the zipper in place, stitching along each side of the zipper and working three or four stitches across the bottom end of the zipper to secure it.

Use a sewing machine with a zipper foot to insert a zipper.

Seams & Hems

To transform your patchwork panel into a finished item, you will need to combine it with other fabrics. This will require machine- and sometimes hand-stitched seams.

Seams and seam allowances

Most of the seams used in the projects in this book are sewn using a sewing machine as this will give a hard-wearing seam. If you want to complete an item by hand, you can work the seams using a backstitch (see page 123).

The instructions will tell you the width of the seam allowance—the margin between the stitching and the raw edge of the fabric.

Sometimes you will need to clip into the seam to help the fabric to curve around or into a complicated shape (see page 115). On other occasions, you may trim the seam allowance so that it is not bulky, especially at the corners. Take care not to cut too close to, or into, the stitching or your seams will unravel.

Double-turned hem

A double-turned hem is used in a number of the projects. It will give you a nicely finished edge, which is ideal when the hem will be visible on the finished project (for example, on the ends of ties and backs of pillows).

To create a double-turned hem, fold the edge of the fabric and fold over to the wrong side by ½ in. (1.25cm) and iron a crease to hold it in position. Repeat the process on the same edge, folding again by ½ in. (1.25cm) to hide the raw edge of the fabric; then press and pin into position. Baste the hem, remove the pins and stitch along the top (inner) edge of your fold to secure.

Trimming a seam allowance will make the finished seam less bulky.

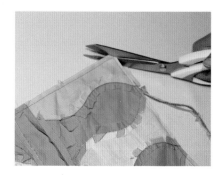

Removing the seam allowance helps to create sharp corners.

A double-turned hem allows you to hide the raw edge of the fabric.

Ladder stitch

This stitch is used to close the gap in a seam so that the stitches do not show. It is sometimes also called slip, blind, or hidden stitch. Use a thread in a color that coordinates with the fabric (a contrasting color has been used in the photograph to show the stitches).

Tuck in the seam allowance (you may find it helpful to baste it into place). Thread your needle and knot the end of the thread. Insert the needle from the wrong to the right side of the fabric, so the knot is hidden inside one of the folds in the seam.

You can pin the edges to hold the seam together, or just use your fingers to align the edges.

Working into the folded edges of the fabric, insert the needle into the opposite side of the seam from where you started and bring it out again ¼ in. (0.5cm) on the same folded edge. Pull the thread tight every two or three stitches (if you do it after each one it will be hard to insert the needle for the next stitch).

Insert the needle into the first side of the seam, opposite where it last came out, working from front to back. Bring the needle back to the front on the same side and ¼ in. (0.5cm) from where it went in. Continue to stitch in this way until the seam is complete.

Make a final stitch, pushing the needle through the loop in the thread to make a knot. For extra security, repeat to make a second knot. To hide the end of the thread, draw it into fabric, pull it tight and then cut it close to the fabric surface so that it snaps back out of view.

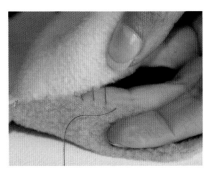

Use a ladder stitch when you do not want your stitches to show.

Embroidery

Patchwork and appliqué provide the perfect canvas for hand or machine embroidery. You can use decorative stitches to outline shapes or add details to them.

You can embellish your projects with embroidery. If you want to use your sewing machine to do this, you will need to use the same type of thread as your hand sewing. If you choose to embroider by hand, you will need embroidery floss. For hand embroidery you will also need an embroidery (or crewel) needle. This has a sharp point and slightly elongated eye that makes it easier to thread with floss.

As with all threads, you will find that better-quality thread is sold in more vibrant colors and it less likely to break while you sew with it.

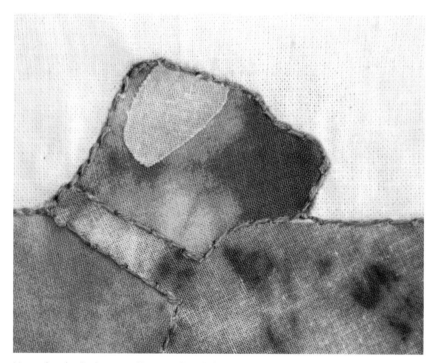
Use a backstitch to outline appliqué shapes.

Running stitch

This simple stitch is used for basting, but it also can be used for embroidery. It is ideal for outlining shapes or adding line details.

Bring the needle and thread from the back to the front of the fabric and the point where you want to start stitching and pull it through.

Insert the needle from the front to the back of the fabric ¼ in. (0.5cm) to the right of where it emerged and pull the thread through. You have made one stitch.

Bring the needle and thread back to the front ¼ in. (0.5cm) to the right of where you last inserted it. Repeat as desired.

You can also use running stitch to baste your seams.

Backstitch

This stitch can be used to outline designs.

Working from right to left, bring the needle and thread from the back to the front of the fabric, one stitch length from the point where you want to start stitching, and pull it through.

Insert the needle at the point at which you want the stitching to start and bring it back out one stitch length ahead of the first stitch. Return the needle to the back of the fabric through the same hole as the end of the first stitch. Repeat as desired until the line of stitches is complete.

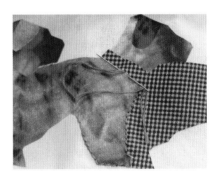

Backstitch creates a neat finish along edges and to add details.

continued on page 124

French knots create decorative beads of thread.

French knot

Bring your needle from the back to the front of the fabric at the point where you want to make the French knot.

With the needle in your dominant hand and held flat on the fabric, use the fingers of your other hand to hold the embroidery floss to one side.

Loop the floss around the needle two or three times, using your nondominant hand to pull the floss tight around the needle.

Hold the floss in place while you return the needle to the back of the fabric, as close as possible to the point from which it emerged.

Slowly pull the needle through the fabric and then pull it tight to form the knot.

Take care to work the satin stitches close together, so they cover the surface of the fabric.

Satin stitch

This flat, filling stitch can be used to decorate small areas of fabric. You may find it helpful to draw the outline of the space you want to fill with tailor's chalk or an erasable fabric pen before you begin.

Insert the needle from the back to the front of the fabric at the point where you want to make your first stitch.

Insert the needle from the front to the back of the fabric on the opposite side of the shape.

Insert the needle from the back to the front of the fabric, at the side of the shape where you began, and then return it to the back of the fabric on the opposite side.

Repeat until the shape is filled in, keeping the stitches close together and taking care not to pull the thread too tight or the fabric will pucker.

Index

A

Angelfish Brush Roll 48–51

appliqué 116

apron 30–33

B

backstitch 120, 123

bags

Hedgehog Project Bag 70–73

Labrador Tote Bag 12–15

ball-headed pins 105

basting 112–113

external corners 113

external curves 113

internal corners 113

internal curves 113

straight edges 113

basting stitch 113

basting thread 102

Bird Place Mat 96–99

blanket 78–81

brush roll 48–51

bulletin board 84–87

buttons 118

C

Cat and Mouse Clock 24–27

Cat Pillow Cover 16–19

Chicken Apron 30–33

clock 24–27

corners 113, 114

Cow Tea Cozy 38–41

curved seams 113, 115, 120

cutting out 109–111

on the bias 111

fabric quantity 109, 110–111

on the grain 111

number of shapes, calculating 109, 110

D

documents portfolio 66–69

double-turned hems 120

E

Elephant Bulletin Board 84–87

embroidery 122–124

backstitch 123

French knots 124

machine embroidery 102, 122

running stitch 123

satin stitch 124

embroidery foot 104

F

fabric scissors 105

fabric shapes

basting 112–113

cutting out 109–111

handpiecing 114–115

fabric-marking pens 105

fabrics 106–107

100 percent cotton 106

choosing 8, 106

patterned fabrics 107, 111

plain fabrics 106

precut pieces (fat quarters) 111

prewashing 106

quantities, calculating 110–111

tightly woven fabrics 106

waste 9

fastenings 118–119
  buttons 118
  press studs/snap fasteners 119
  Velcro 119
  zippers 119
fat quarters 111
feed dogs 104
finishing off 116–117
  appliqué 116
  pressing 117
  quilting 117
  topstitching 117
Fox Seat Pad 74–77
French knots 124
fusible webbing 116

G
Goldfish Journal Cover 56–59

H
handpiecing 114–115
  arranging shapes 114
  corners 114
  curved seams 115
  removing cardboard shapes 115
  straight edges, joining 114
  whipstitch 114
Hedgehog Project Bag 70–73
Horse Wall Hanging 42–45
hot pad 60–63

J
journal cover 56–59

L
Labrador Tote Bag 12–15
ladder stitch 121
Lizard Pillow 92–95

M
mats
  Bird Place Mat 96–99
  Sheep Play Mat 34–37
Monkey Tablet Sleeve 88–91

N
needles
  embroidery (crewel) needles 122
  hand-sewing needles 103

O
Owl Portfolio 66–69

P
Penguin Hot Pad 60–63
pillows
  Cat Pillow Cover 16–19
  Fox Seat Pad 74–77
  Lizard Pillow 92–95
  Scottie Dog Bolster Pillow 20–23
pins 105
  ball-headed pins 105
  quilter's pins 105
place mat 96–99
play mat 34–37
press studs/snap fasteners 119
pressing 117

Q
quilter's pins 105
quilting 117

R
rotary cutter 105
running stitch 123

S

satin stitch 124

scissors 105

   fabric scissors 105

   general-purpose scissors 105

Scottie Dog Bolster Pillow 20–23

seam ripper 105

seams 120

   clipping and trimming 113, 120

   curved seams 113, 115, 120

   ladder stitch 121

   pressing 117

   seam allowance 9, 111, 112, 120

seat pad 74–77

sewing machine 104

sewing thread 103

sharps 103

Sheep Play Mat 34–37

stool cover 52–55

T

tablet sleeve 88–91

tailor's chalk 105

tape measure and ruler 105

tea cozy 38–41

Teddy Bear Blanket 78–81

templates 108

   cutting templates 9, 108

   enlarging 108

   making 108

   sewing templates 9, 108

   thickness 9, 108

tessellated shapes 6

threads 102–103

   basting thread 102

   embroidery thread 122

   sewing thread 103

   thread length 103

tools and equipment 102–105

   fabric-marking pens 105

   needles 103

   pins 105

   rotary cutter 105

   scissors 105

   seam ripper 105

   sewing machine 104

   tailor's chalk 105

   tape measure and ruler 105

   threads 102–103

topstitching 117

Turtle Stool Cover 52–55

V

Velcro 119

W

wall hanging 42–45

whipstitch 114

Z

zipper foot 104

zippers 119

Resources

You can find all the fabrics and notions you need at your favorite craft and fabric stores. You can also find them at these online retailers.

US

Amazon
www.amazon.com

Etsy
www.etsy.com

Hochanda TV
www.hochanda.com

Jo-Ann Stores Inc
www.joann.com

Michael's
www.michaels.com

Pat Catan's
www.patcatans.com

UK

Amazon
www.amazon.co.uk

Craft Yourself Silly
www.craftyourselfsilly.com

Etsy
www.etsy.com

Hobbycraft
www.hobbycraft.co.uk

Hochanda TV
www.hochanda.com

Acknowledgments

Thanks to my Auntie Sue, Nan (grandma) and Auntie Kathy for introducing me to sewing. I would also like to thank Heather for helping me to sew some of the samples—without her basting skills this book might never have happened! Neil our photographer was so patient with the step-by-step photographs and allowed me to mess up his studio. I must also thank Matt for his support and help cutting out many random shapes and putting up with lots of late night sewing and pins on the floor.